JUGGERNAUTS

THE MAKING OF A RUNNER & A TEAM
IN THE FIRST AMERICAN RUNNING BOOM

STEVE ADKISSON

Outskirts Press, Inc.
Denver, Colorado

Outskirts Press, Inc.
http://www.outskirtspress.com

ISBN: 978-1-4327-3339-1

Library of Congress Control Number: 2008938888

Outskirts Press and the "OP" logo are trademarks belonging to Outskirts Press, Inc.

PRINTED IN THE UNITED STATES OF AMERICA

FOREWORD

By Bob Roncker, founder and owner of Bob Roncker's Running Spot and 2007 inductee into the Running Retailer Association Hall of Fame for his long time contributions to the sport of running.

September 16, 2008

There is something magical about the year 1972 for runners in America. If you were already among that cadre of individuals who considered themselves distance runners or if you were contemplating rising from the couch and taking up the sport for the first time, you may have realized that you were both witnessing and taking a role in an intoxicating and unique era as it applied to distance running. At the highest levels of competition Americans more than held their own against the best that the other continents had to offer. These successes in high sport that the USA enjoyed were short-lived. They disappeared with the arrival of the 1980s. For over two decades we struggled to match strides with the influx of African runners. Only now, after this long hiatus, are American distance runners fancying themselves competitive at the Olympics and World Championships. However, back then not only was there enthusiasm for distance running at the apex of the sport, there was also a tremendous influx of everyday average individuals who wished to align themselves with this physical activity. A variety of happenings occurred to cause a gentle ripple to become a swell and then a tsunami.

In the early 1960s Bill Bowerman, the track and field coach at the University of Oregon, introduced a new concept that he had recently learned in New Zealand. He coauthored a 90-page book entitled *Jogging*. In it a schedule leading to fitness was formulated. Then, Kenneth H. Cooper, M.D., who at the time was an Air Force Colonel, published a book in 1968 that was called "Aerobics." This book illustrated how various aerobic pursuits could be simply compared by assigning them a certain number of "aerobic points" based upon the duration of the activity. Finally, many citizens were able to witness on television Frank Shorter's inspirational marathon victory during the 1972 Munich Olympics. We all love and need good role models. There he was. We could see him capturing the first Olympic marathon gold medal by an American in 64 years. What couldn't we achieve? This performance proved to be a catalyst that catapulted many Americans to entertain the thought of running as a source of pleasure and satisfaction.

Before, running, often in the form of laps, had been punishment meted out by coaches for transgressions in a sport, usually one involving a ball. Reading the sayings on the back of tee shirts worn by high school cross country team members as they warm up for their race is an entertaining sideline, sometimes rivaling the race itself. One of my favorite quotes, and one always worn with great pride, is, "Our sport is your punishment." Indeed, running was becoming so popular that Jim Fixx's book, *The Complete Book of Running* remained #1 on the New York Times nonfiction best seller list for 11 weeks in 1978.

It is in this context, during this particular period of time, when no achievement or goal was too outlandish or far out of reach not to be seriously considered that the author of *Juggernauts,* ninth grader Steve Adkisson, began his running career in 1972. Many school aged distance runners entered the sport either because they failed to make the cut for another squad or they were using running to better prepare themselves for another activity. That happened to me. I started running in the fall of 1958 during my sophomore year in high school when the basketball coach started up a cross country team to get his players in shape. Steve's motivation was similar because he also considered himself a "hooper."

The chapters simply flow. We witness the gradual development of an individual and a team. In the beginning neither gave reason for other competitors, individuals or school teams to be overly concerned. One of the true values of distance running is the establishment of and the striving to attain goals. Personal and team goals remain paramount in this story, but I sense something else happening. Running becomes more intrinsic. The mere act of running becomes the reward itself. However, don't be mislead and think that this is a Rocky type story full of "all work and no play."

Boy, did they know how to play. *Juggernauts* spans Steve's four years of high school. Many of their adventures should be cataloged as only to be known about by coaches or parents after many years have passed. I for one was envious after reading about the various escapades that the team members had together. Why didn't we do some of those things when we were in school? The various connections, coach-athlete, teammate-teammate, friend-friend, and runner- competitor, demonstrate many levels of relationships. I found *Juggernauts* to be a very compelling book that I did not wish to set down. Reading it touched me. I laughed and I cried.

I have known Steve since the mid 1980s. For some time

he has been making references to this book that he was writing. Well, it's completed now and I have to say that it is one of the most enjoyable books centered on running that I have ever read.

. . . Little sister
Just remember
As you wander through the blue
The little kite
That you sent flying
On a Sunday afternoon
Made of something light as nothing
Made of joy that matters too
How the little dreams we dream
Are all we can really do . . .

-Patty Griffin
Kite Song
Impossible Dream

I
FRESHMAN

KENTUCKY
AUGUST 1972

My first day at Lloyd Memorial High School had gone pretty well for me right up to the Afternoon Announcements. I'd found all six of my classrooms and been introduced to my Biology, English, Math, PE, History, and Typing classes. I had a pretty clear idea of what was expected of me and I even enjoyed the school lunch despite all the griping my fellow students had done about it. Sitting in homeroom waiting for dismissal, I sat quietly with my stack of new books when the principal hit the switch and bumped the microphone a couple of times with his index finger. The school intercom system squawked as he adjusted the microphone. He read the names of the students who had earned after-school detention already. He announced the upcoming football game against Dixie High School, and then as almost an afterthought, read from a note the new coach had left for him: "Any student interested in trying out for cross-country should report to the commons immediately after school."

I asked my friend Terry if he knew what this was.

"It's the fall sport all the basketball players do to get in shape for basketball season," Terry answered.

I really didn't understand the concept of getting-in-shape for something. My entire existence up to this point had been spent in motion. If there had been a diagnosis for any of the hyperactive kid disorders then, I would have been the poster boy. From playing dawn-to-dusk baseball in the neighborhood sandlots, reenacting the last three wars in the trenches of our local woods, hunting with my dad and brothers, to riding my bike everywhere that was too far to walk, I had probably never sat still long enough to have a measurable resting heartrate. I only watched television on Saturday mornings in the winter, and only then if the cartoons were funny.

At 5' 2" and with every intention of soon breaking 100 pounds, I was an aspiring hooper who spent most of my spare time between October and April out on the neighborhood concrete basketball courts. With the idea of gaining an advantage on the kids I knew who played football and spent most of their fall standing around at football practice, I decided right away to show up for the cross-country meeting. It was one of the most profound impulsive decisions I ever made in my life. Looking back on it, I think the real reason I went was because Terry also told me they gave out uniforms to everybody who ran, and it was an easy way to earn a varsity letter. Usually there were only 7 kids who stayed on the team for the whole season. Besides that, I had to wait for my older brother to finish his meetings after school and our ride home from school had told us he would be late. I figured I might as well wait out in the commons for them.

Much to the surprise of everyone, including the coach, about 15 boys milled around in front of the school waiting for the meeting while the rest of the students filed out heading for home. Several of the upper classmen joked among themselves, ignoring the rest of us. Most wore bell bottom pants, long hair, army jackets, and a couple of them smoked as we waited for the coach to arrive.

Coach Daley was brand new to the area, having taken a

4

vacated junior high PE job over the summer. He was fresh out of college after his tour of Vietnam and then obtaining his degree under the GI Bill. Coach Daley strolled up to the group with his clipboard in hand and a whistle around his neck. He was tall and stoutly built, an ex football player who looked like he could still put a hurting on somebody if need be. His blondish hair was cut close with a modest comb over of his receding hair line.

"Now fellas, I only have a few simple rules," he began. "And the first one is the most important – Show Up On Time. I expect you to be dressed, stretched out, and ready to run no later than 10 minutes after school lets out. I promise you we will get along fine as long as you follow my instructions."

"Rule number two is The Golden Rule, and by that I mean let's all get along. We've got some seniors here and some freshmen, and a few in between. I'm new here too so I have a lot to learn. I'll be fair with you, and I expect you to be fair with me and with each other. Those of you who have run before can offer a lot to the new guys. Don't be afraid to step up and give advice to these younger fellas."

What none of us knew at the time was that even though this was his very first teaching and head coaching job, he had done his student teaching and been a coach at a school in Dexter, Missouri that was the home of the Missouri state cross-country champion. Even though innovation was not necessarily in his bag of tricks, Coach Daley had a natural acumen for understanding physical training programs and had paid attention to what had made this Missouri kid a state record holder in every distance event from the 880 to the two mile. The Missouri school had not had a cross country team and some of the students there asked Coach Daley to coach them. He had designed a training program for those students after doing a lot of reading and studying on the sport and he was about to start implementing it on us.

He told us what gear we would need - shorts, socks, shoes, a towel and a tee shirt- and that if we knew anyone else who was interested in running to bring them to practice tomorrow.

That night at home I rolled up some gym shorts in a towel. I wore the socks and shoes and tee shirt I planned to run in to school anyway so I figured I was all set. I told my mom I was going out for cross-country and she said fine, what time would I be home for supper?

That first practice took place on a Friday, and the football team had its first game that night, so coach knew better than to expect too much out of us. He was probably anxious to get home and eat dinner so he could get back up to school for the game himself.

Of the fifteen guys who had shown up for the after school meeting, there were twelve of us who showed up for the first practice. Other than Terry, I only knew one of the other guys on the team. Coach went around and asked each of us our names and I tried hard to remember them, but I knew it would be a while before I would be confident of putting the right name with the right face. Matt Huff was a sophomore and had a confidence and pleasant demeanor that made him memorable. He was maybe 5' 7" and slightly built with dark hair and dark eyes. Gary Graves had long red hair, lamb chop sideburns and was one of just a couple of seniors on the team, so he stood out. Rick Murr, who we called Roy, lived near my house and we had played baseball and basketball together for several years. Steve Nienaber was another sophomore, tall and long legged. He wore thick black glasses and had short curly hair and long sideburns. He had a way of smiling out of the side of his mouth that seemed like he was hiding something. The others I would have to work on remembering.

Coach wrote down our names as we gave them out and then he set his clipboard down. He instructed one of the two seniors on the team to guide us around the 1-mile course that snaked through the school grounds. The course was pretty easy to understand but we all jogged along in that quiet manly feeling-out of the others' skills and strength. I didn't recognize this was what we were doing until many hundred runs later, but as a snot-nosed freshman, I knew my place in the hierarchy that is established when a pack is forming. A few of the more experienced guys sped up a little near the end of the first lap (to impress the coach I was already figuring out). Coach said "Go around again," and he glanced at his stop watch.

I ran comfortably in the pack and worked up a little sweat on the second lap. The high school cross-country race distance in Kentucky was two-miles at the time, so when we were finished I thought two-miles were pretty easy.

The second day stands out as one of those landmark days in a boy's life that shapes the way he travels the world for the rest of his days. Knowing little about the Friday night party habits of senior high school students in 1972, Terry and I were a little surprised to be the first ones to arrive for the 8:00 a.m. Saturday practice. Coach was sitting on the hood of his car when we rolled up on our bikes. He had a towel around his neck and was holding a cup of coffee while looking over the morning newspaper. He nodded hello to us but I was pretty sure he had not learned our names yet.

The other dozen or so runners milled in and the last one to arrive was one of the longhaired, cigarette-smoking guys. In the days before the proliferation of sports drinks, it was pretty much anything goes for quenching thirst. One of the runners whose dad had dropped him off toted a 16 oz bottle of Barq's Red Pop and the senior leader of the team roared around the corner on two wheels of his 64 Comet with half a minute to spare and finishing the last of a 16 oz bottle of Pepsi as he stepped out of the car.

This made an impression on Coach and I don't think it was one that improved his mood much. At 8:00 sharp, Coach marched across the parking lot and opened the gate to the track / football field. The track at our school was one of the last remaining cinder tracks in the area, and although cinders are an excellent and forgiving surface if they are properly maintained by raking and rolling, ours was normally ignored from the last home track meet in May until it was time to prep it for the first meets in late March of the following year. In August, it had a groove dug into it on the inside lane from the football players running "laps" of punishment in their cleats. This rut was about 6 inches deep and easily avoided if you wanted to run a comfortable distance outside of it.

When everyone was assembled, Coach had us sit down on the infield grass while he gave us the first of many educational explanations about what we were going to be doing.

"Fellas, today we are going to do an interval workout. There are three or four types of training we are going to do over the course of the year. What we did yesterday is called Long Slow Distance or L.S.D. Even though you only ran 2 miles yesterday, it was done at an easy pace. We'll gradually increase that to where eventually you'll run 8 or 10 miles. That might seem really far to most of you right now, but by the time the season is over you will be able to do it.

"The second kind of training we'll do is called fartlek, which is a Swedish word which translates into 'speed play'. Basically it means you do a continuous run where you go between slow running and fast running without stopping, but you use slower running to recover between the harder, faster running.

"On our easy days we will do recovery running which will be shorter easier runs that allows your body to work out the stiffness from a hard workout or a race.

"Today's workout is going to be an interval workout. This type of workout is probably the most important and the most difficult for any runner. What we'll do is run a measured distance at a target pace, and then rest a certain amount of time before starting another run. Each run we call a 'repetition' and the rest in between is called the 'interval'."

Coach had us run an easy one mile "warmup" which did the trick on this particularly hot and humid late summer morning. Coach led us in some stretching exercises for a few minutes and then said that today's workout was going to be 10 x 440. Somebody asked him how many times around was a 440 and he said "one" in a tone combining both patience and agitation, which I figured must have been something he picked up in the Army.

Then we all lined up at the top of the straight away and coach said for the first time of what would easily be measured in the thousands for me: "Set . . . Go!"

A couple of the eager young runners bolted off at what was a surprisingly fast pace for me, but I gassed it up and found myself in the middle of the pack as we rounded the first turn and headed down the backstretch. Most of the runners stayed wide of the rut in the inside lane, but a couple of the faster guys were positioning themselves to get an inside shot at the second turn. I was running comfortably along when out of my peripheral vision I saw a body flying at forty-five degrees followed by the fist and extended arm of the biggest guy on the team, the owner of the Comet.

"Don't you ever cut me off again!" were the first words, other than his name, I ever heard come out of the mouth of Gary Graves. He said this as the other kid's body landed on its shoulder and rolled in the gravelly cinders right in front of me and I jumped up and over him as he came to a skidding stop. A little gap opened up around Gary and I was introduced to the concept of the "space" each runner claims.

We finished this first quarter mile and coach seemed pleased with our time. He asked what happened and Gary said he'd been cut off and Coach told us not to do that anymore and that was pretty much the end of it. The runner who was knocked down had jumped back up and finished the lap only a few seconds behind. He was Roy Murr, the sophomore who lived in my neighborhood. I knew him to be a very nice and easy going guy so I was a little surprised to see his steely-eyed tight-lipped determination building up in him as we walked in a big circle during the 60 seconds "interval" of rest coach said we had before the next 440.

"Set . . . Go!"

Off we went again, this time a little faster than the first one. Roy got the hole shot on the first turn and kept the inside position down the back straight as the others sped up to reel him back in. Matt, a sophomore who had run the year before cruised in to the lead with Roy and Gary close behind. As we headed into the second turn, I experienced those first signs of burning in my lungs as I tried my best to keep up.

We rolled out of the second turn pretty much in single file, but all within a few seconds of each other. Matt was a few strides ahead of everybody but Gary got up a little speed to catch and pass Roy in the final few strides.

"That's two," Coach said as we all finished and walked in an even smaller circle than before. What little small talk had been going on before was completely gone as we all sucked in air with our hands clasped behind our heads. I was already sweating.

"Set . . . Go!"

This one caught me by surprise and I found myself having to sprint all the way through the first turn to catch up. Again, Matt and Murr had taken the early lead but Gary was right on their heels. This time Steve Nienaber sped up to the lead group, looking like he was wanting to get in on the action. As I watched the dogfight going on out in front, it occurred to me this would have been a fun thing to watch if it didn't hurt so bad to participate in. This is cool, I thought, ten mini-races in one day of practice.

Those four got out ahead of the rest of us and seemed to be sprinting down the home straight as I came into the last 100 yards. The burn was back and I finished wondering if I could do this seven more times. Many of my teammates didn't bother to walk the rest interval this time, and just stood near the starting line. A couple slumped forward with their hands down on their knees until coach told them to "Keep moving or you'll get tied up." I wanted no part of being tied up.

We did the next several repeats at a little more civil pace. With each one I found it harder and harder to keep up with the front runners, but I also saw that I was not losing ground by much and I was beating many of the others.

"Set . . . Go!"

Just as we finished the ninth 440, the kid named Conrad who had gotten out of the car drinking a Barq's Red Pop, reached a point of exertion that I would eventually come to know myself in future efforts. The combination of overheating, running as fast as possible, and getting caught up in the competition of the workout, had put his body in the position of displaying its rebellion in the ultimate form of purging itself. His projectile vomiting of a vile red fluid was a display worthy of praise in any special effects in the movies. Coach wasn't the only one whose first thought was that this kid was throwing up several pints of his own blood. The coagulated plasma formed in red chunks as it rolled across the dry cinders.

What happened next was what I would describe as one of those life lessons that come to us by the simple process of being where the action is. Coach took the towel he had brought with him and wiped Conrad's face and mouth. He asked him if he was all right, and Conrad answered to my astonishment, "I feel a lot better now." A sanguine smile returned to his flushed face and he walked back towards the starting line.

"Last one. Set . . . Go!" coach said at the same 60 second interval we had maintained for the entire workout.

Without having much time to process all that my 14-year-old eyes had just seen, I took off with the group and we all seemed somewhat fresher as we ran our final round of the track. The last one was probably the fastest 440 of the day although coach hadn't told us what any of the times were. It just felt like we were all covering the ground with a different and newfound efficiency and I had no idea where mine had come from. We finished in a pretty tight group and coach said to walk a whole lap, then jog another mile to cool down.

By the time we had walked a lap, conversations had picked up again. Gary told Roy he was sorry if he hurt him, but no way was he gonna get cut off.

Roy said, "No biggie," and smiled while he lightly brushed some more cinders from the still bleeding wound on his elbow.

Matt jogged on ahead of the rest of us and kept going. I was amazed that anyone could run as hard as we had just run and still be able to do more.

Coach had brought a big cooler of water and when we finished our mile cool down we stood around the cooler filling the little white cone-shaped water cups and drinking the ice cold water. Coach also handed out salt tablets and most of the runners took them. I had never been able to swallow pills so I just pretended not to need any.

Coach passed out some forms for us to take home for our parents to sign, and then said he would see us at practice Monday after school. I think he had us do this Saturday workout just to see how interested anybody was in being on the team. He figured anybody who would show up on a Saturday morning to run a hard workout must really want to do it.

I think he was also trying to determine where we were as far as our fitness was concerned, so he could set up future workout times and paces and know what to expect from us. He was also getting a glimpse at the competitive fire and drive of the ten kids who showed up for practice. It didn't really occur to me then that he must have been pleasantly surprised by what he'd seen in us during this first workout. The next several years would leave him no doubt he was right in his first impression.

Lloyd Memorial High School in 1972 was the kind of place where most of the students who drove cars backed them into the parking spots. I remember hearing my dad and other adults saying they preferred to back their car into a spot because it was easier on a warmed up transmission to go into reverse, and it was also safer to pull out into traffic than to back out. The high school drivers backed in for three different reasons. Some did it so they'd be ready for a quick getaway when school let out, some to hide expired license plates from patrolling police, and some because they never knew when they'd need to jump start their cars.

With a student body of about 800, Lloyd was big enough to have its share of trouble, but small enough for a good faculty and administration to control it.

As a mostly blue collar community, Erlanger had a population that supported education and was involved in every aspect of the school, from sports boosters groups to parents who volunteered every day to prepare and serve food at the cafeteria. The faculty was a good mixture of older experienced teachers and enthusiastic young teachers, most of whom took great pride in doing their job well.

At school on Monday morning I recognized a few more faces. My teammates all acknowledged me in some way or another when we met in the halls, and even though it was just the third day of classes, I was starting to get the feeling I was figuring some things out. My freshman English teacher, Ms. Hart, had given us a list of books we would read and had assigned *Adventures of Huckleberry Finn*, a book I had already read and enjoyed.

I was a slow reader, but I comprehended well. I figured I was already a little bit ahead of the game. My brother Bill had told me that if I paid attention in class and did all the assignments on time, I would not have any trouble passing all my classes. I did just ok with Math, but in the first few days I could tell from the questions being asked by my classmates that I was going to be all right.

Science and History were mostly reading assignments and class lectures and would be graded with tests and quizzes that could easily be passed if you read the chapters and listened to the lectures. The elective class I had was Typing I and since I had never even tried to use a typewriter, I thought this would be a challenge. After the first few classes, I had mastered typing " a s d f j k l ; ." The teacher, Mrs. Blankenbaker, was very patient and thorough, so I

14

started to gain confidence. A couple of my friends made fun of me for being in a "girl class" but I was too late when I tried to sign up for the popular "Shop" class and the only elective left was this typing class. I was determined to make the best of it.

Throughout the day, I kept thinking about the Saturday cross-country workout and I was looking forward to practice when the last bell rang.

Lloyd Memorial High School circa 1972
Spectator Yearbook photo.

STEVE ADKISSON

"What would life be like if we had no courage
to attempt anything?"

-Vincent Van Gogh (1853-1890)

I started keeping a "Runners Log" early in my freshman
year. I used a blank ledger book some older relative had
given to me that is six inches wide and eighteen inches tall,
with large bold letters on the front that simply read DAY. It
has columns that I labeled for dates, description of workout, weight, and miles run. It contains goals for the individual months and different seasons. Sometimes it is hard to
look back at it and make sense of what I had written down.
I know that it tells the truth as I knew it at the time. Race
times are often noted in the $1/100^{th}$ of seconds. Miles read
like the car odometer used to measure the routes we ran in
tenths of a mile. Names, race places, and team finishes are
all specific. My daily penciled entries tell a great deal about
what I learned from my first days of running until I graduated. The description column became a diary of not only
how hard the workouts were but also a documentary of how
running was impacted by all the other things going on in
the world.

The idea of keeping a log came from a magazine article
I had read in *Runner's World*, a little magazine that my
neighbor, Kent Rea, had loaned to me when he heard I was
running cross-country. I didn't know it at the time, but Mr.
Rea would become a very important influence on my running career by sharing his knowledge and experience with
me.

Kent Rea lived a couple houses down the road from us.
He was the director of our local YMCA and he and his wife
Mary were good friends of my parents. The Rea's had three

16

children the same ages as some of my younger brothers and sisters so our families spent time together. Kent had been a runner for many years, in an era before the running boom, and had completed marathons. He was a daily runner and proponent of fitness for all as his position with the YMCA would suggest. He was also very generous in his willingness to share his experience and what resources he could, such as the magazine, with my friends and me. His gentle nudges of encouragement guided me in ways he probably never considered and that I probably never fully appreciated at the time. It is amazing how small a spark it takes sometimes to kindle a fire.

On September 9th, just a few weeks into my first season as a runner, I watched on television as Frank Shorter won the Munich Olympic Marathon and Steve Prefontaine had run his amazing 5,000 meters, finishing fourth after pulling the field through a sub 4:00 minute last mile, as a 21 year old. The games were marred by terrorists' killing and kidnapping of Israeli athletes, bringing the world's attention not only to the events of the Olympics, but to the horrors of a new kind of terrorism. Shorter's victory would lead a whole new generation of Americans into distance running and was a catalyst of the fitness boom which began around the same time. As the first American to win an Olympic Marathon in 64 years, Shorter brought together an attitude of discipline and playfulness to a sport often thought of as an activity for masochists. The publicity of his victory came at an ideal time for me since I was just gaining a hunger for information about running. There was no end to magazine articles, newspaper stories, and television coverage of how he trained, what he ate, and what it took to become a champion.

My freshman logbook was pretty rudimentary in that it doesn't mention much beyond the mileage, times, and my

17

finish place in the races. The first entries read:

August 26 2 miles
August 27 Warmup 1 mile. 10 440's Conrad puked
August 28 Sunday. Ran home from church ? miles legs
  sore
August 29 Warmup 1 mile 20 bleachers Run 1 mile
  Time Trial 5:40

I was, apparently, sucked in to the sport from my very first step. In the first week, the logbook mentions "legs sore", but they were apparently not sore enough to justify taking a day off.

After less than a full week of practice, it was time for our first race. Coach had decided that rather than do a team practice race, we would just use the first "Dual Meet" to determine who our top 7 runners would be in the meets to follow. One of the most competitive cross-country teams in Northern Kentucky, Bishop Brossart High School, bussed their runners to the Lloyd Memorial campus for the after-school meet.

The race distance for cross-country in Kentucky at the time was 2 miles, although I remember Coach quoting the rulebook as "approximately 2 miles". We would find out later that not every course was measured to any degree of accuracy. Our home course was a carefully measured 1-mile loop that we covered twice. This loop was a modified figure 8 incorporating the modest hill in the front yard of the school. There were a couple of short hills to make it challenging, but mostly it was flat and fast. Large trees marked most of our turns and the turn furthest from the start was around the backstop of the practice baseball field of the Junior High School. Just beyond that turn, the course went into the woods for about 100 yards where a fallen tree was an obstacle to jump over each time we came to it.

Before this first meet, our team went out and, as became a ritual for us at each meet afterwards, walked the course. This served as a way to loosen up, prepare a strategy for the race, and learn the fine, ubiquitous art of talking smack. As we walked together down the long beginning straightaway, we passed the other team grouped together in the shade of a large maple tree. I experienced for the first time that combination of fear and excitement that is often described as "butterflies." I, of course, thought this feeling which brought together a blend of nausea, inability to speak, and shaky hands, was limited only to me. Seeing the older runners from the other team stretching and getting themselves mentally prepared for something they had vast experience at, I was completely awestruck. Bishop Brossart had competed in the State Meet the previous year, and our Coach had told us two of their seniors had been mentioned as being contenders for the individual state championship. I studied them as we walked by.

My teammate Gary Graves was also a senior and he had competed against these runners for each of his previous three seasons. I had only known Gary for six days at the time of this first race and had barely spoken to him. Gary had shoulder length red hair, long side burns, and was probably our largest runner at 5'11 and 140 pounds. As the most experienced runner on the team, those of us who were brand new flocked around him to hear what he had to say about running in a real race.

Gary Graves 1972
Spectator Yearbook photo.

Just as we were passing the green and white clad Brossart runners, Gary raised his voice just a little and said, "Man, I'm beat from that long run yesterday." We walked on out of hearing range from the Brossart runners and several of us looked at him as if we were wondering if he had run some more after practice had ended, something that would never cross my mind. I had only run "2 miles easy" according to my logbook.

Terry, one of the other freshmen, asked him, "Did you run more after pract...?"

"No, you goofball," Gary interrupted. "I did the same workout as you. I just said that so those other guys would think we were all tired and didn't know any better than to do a hard run the day before a meet."

I was glad I hadn't been the one to ask, but the light

bulb was starting to flicker in my head. If the other runners were overconfident about being able to beat us, it would give us a chance to surprise them a little. It would take a year or two of practice for me to learn the art of knowing just the right thing to say or do, but I had some very astute teachers in the art of getting in the head of the opponent.

Gary led us around the rest of the loop and when we all got into single file on the trail which went a short distance through the woods, he began to jog. We all followed his lead and ran the last half of the course, which we already knew, and didn't really need to study. Near the end, we grouped up to jog in the last few hundred yards together.

After we stretched and ran a few 100-yard pickups, Coach called us over to where he was standing near the starting line. We huddled around him, a little away from the other team and the few parents and handful of student spectators assembled near the starting line.

Coach looked around the group and kind of smiled. I think he was as nervous about his first meet as a head coach as I was about running it.

He said "Fellas. Now, you've got nothing to lose. Nobody is expecting us to do much this first time out, so if we just keep them in sight we will be doing respectably. Some of you have never raced before so just remember you need to have a full step in front of another runner to move in front of him. It can get rough in the first couple hundred yards. If you cut somebody off, you could be disqualified, or worse yet – get your leg ripped up by the spikes of the guy you cut off. Try to get out hard and stay in a pack for as long as you can. Remember, the top five will be scored and the top seven will push their first five back if you can finish ahead of any of them. Now, I'm going to leave the huddle and go get my starting pistol so if anybody has anything to say to the team, go ahead. Then everybody get back to the starting line."

Coach left and the huddle shrank a little as everybody came together into a tight circle. Gary, sensing how nervous most of us were and being experienced enough to know you can't run well when your whole body is knotted up in tension, came up with a joke that was over my head about the difference between blondes and brunettes in backseats, but most of the older guys got it and laughed so I laughed with them.

Matt had us put our hands together in the middle and recite the "Lord's Prayer" which I knew the Catholic version of, and when the Catholic version ended and the non-sectarian version continued, I stood dumbfounded. I caught the eyes of one of my friends from Catholic elementary school, and both our brows furrowed in puzzlement.

". . . For thine is the kingdom and the power and the glory, forever and ever. Amen."

I didn't have any time to puzzle this one out, as Gary shouted "Juggs, on three" and counted "One, two, three" and we all shouted "Juggs." We broke from the huddle and headed to the starting line. At the same time, the Mustangs from Bishop Brossart were jogging back from their run out, and all seven of their varsity runners were lean and muscled. Our full squad of twelve was dressed in the same uniforms that had been handed down and reused since about 1965. Several of us were short and skinny freshmen and the oversized uniforms hung loosely off our shoulders. I wore some knee high basketball socks and a pair of black leather spikes like the ones Jesse Owens wore in the 1936 Berlin Olympics. Coach had fished these out for me from a box in the athletic department storage room.

Not having much time to think through any kind of race tactic, when the gun went off to signal the start of the race, I just started running. Over my week of practice, I had heard the term "pace" quite a few times, but I didn't really have much of a feeling for gauging how fast was too fast for racing a distance of two miles. I had already found out that I was pretty fast, when it came to shorter distances like 220 or 440 yards. I was keeping up fairly well with the other runners on my team in practice when we ran shorter intervals. In baseball and basketball, you usually have to run as fast as absolutely possible, but you only have to do it for short bursts. This, I was learning, was something completely different.

The first part of our course was down a long straightway in the grass between the side of the school building and a sidestreet that paralleled the course. It is slightly downhill at the beginning and eases uphill near the first turn. At the end of this 400-yard straightaway, the route did a hairpin right turn around a big maple tree. The sharp turn required you to come almost to a stop as you went around the tree and accelerated again to go down one of the small hills. This first turn, as I would learn over the dozens of races I would run on this course, was a place where a runner could put some distance on his competition. If you could get to the turn first and accelerate hard around the corner and down the hill, you could spread the field out behind you as everybody slowed to negotiate the turn without tripping over each other, or getting tangled up figuring out who had the right of way.

Evidently, some of the Brossart runners already knew this. As we sprinted toward the tree, several of them got out ahead of the rest of us and when one of our lead runners got shoved down trying to round the corner, the rest of the field stopped or ran wide around the turn to avoid the pileup. I got pushed into the tree, then had to back up, and then go around the pile up. By the time I was headed down the hill, there were seven or eight ahead of me and I was already starting to feel the pain of going out too fast.

I ran up the little hill and made the sharp left turn that took us on to a short flat stretch before crossing the driveway to the school. As I turned I looked to my left to see the single file line of most of my teammates and the remaining Brossart runners coming up the hill behind me. We crossed the street and went down a small grade toward the practice baseball field and I could see three of my teammates up ahead chasing after the leaders.

The ball field was dry and dusty and as we ran through the outfield, hundreds of grasshoppers sprang up and scurried off at random as we went by. I thought this was one of the coolest things I had ever seen in my life. It was like Moses parting the waters except everybody was Moses and the grasshoppers' feet tickled when they grabbed onto and then pushed off my skinny legs.

Around the backstop, I ran through the dried dust kicked up by the runners ahead of me. This must be where the term "eat my dust" came from. Breathing in a lung full of this dust only added to the growing discomfort I was experiencing just a half-mile into this two-mile race.

As we entered the short wooded section where the trail was only wide enough for one person at a time, I could feel a group hot on my heels. As soon as the trail opened up, two of my teammates and one of the Brossart runners went by me. I tucked in behind them and gutted out the rest of the first lap hanging on to the back of this group.

Coach was calling out our mile split as we came around to the start/finish line and when I heard him say 5:20, I was pretty amazed to think that we had just run the first mile faster than I had run the one-mile time trial we had run on Monday. My 5:40 'time trial' mile had felt like top speed, and I was sure that I had given everything I had to give. Discovering that I could run even faster than that, and realizing I still had another whole mile to go were two pieces of news I wished had not come to me at the same time.

The group I was running with sort of inhaled after we were out of site of the coaches. When we got back to the first sharp turn on the course, there were five of us all together but no one seemed nearly as anxious to push anybody around as we made the hairpin turn for the second time. This phenomenon that the further you go in a distance race the more polite runners seem to get was something I would remember to ask Gary about after the race was over.

What happened next was something that I will always remember as my first contact with the spiritual side of running. I guess you could call it that. What actually happened was I woke up to discover that my body had covered another half-mile of the course without my brain's knowledge. I was startled to look up and see that I was heading into the final 100 yards of the race when the last I remembered was going around the backstop at the opposite end of the course. If I could not remember covering the distance from there to where I was now, what else was I missing during this brief nihilistic delusion? I felt ok, not like I was in danger of heat stroke or hypoxia or any other physical trouble.

It was more like I was so engrossed in the act of running that I was completely unaware of my surroundings. I had passed one of my teammates and one of the Brossart runners somewhere along the way. I looked ahead and saw the finish line and mustered up the slightest bit of kick I had left.

Coach was busy writing down our times and places and a student volunteer handed me a card with the number "11" written on it when I was through the short chute set up at the finish. I looked around behind me and watched the last two Brossart runners and the rest of our team finish, three or four together and a few stragglers about 30 seconds back. When everyone was finished, Coach came over and took our cards. He went back to the finish area and started writing on the paper in his clipboard. A few minutes later he went to the Bishop Brossart Coach and handed him a piece of paper and shook his hand in congratulations.

I was pretty well recovered from the misery of the last mile and a half of racing when Coach returned to the group and told us Brossart had beaten us, but that our times were "outstanding" for the first meet of the season. I could tell Coach was pleased, even with our loss and I found this very unusual in a coach because in all my previous sporting competitions, losing was always the precursor to a verbal lashing. Coach made us feel proud to have even placed two of our top five before their fifth runner. My 11th place finish was good enough for me to score as our team's fourth runner.

Coach told us to cool down with another lap of the course and as we jogged out to start this lap, the Bishop Brossart runners came along at the same time. Some of the older guys from their team smiled and traded little observations back and forth with the older guys on our team. I tagged quietly along beside my teammates and enjoyed hearing the friendly talk about the race, the coming season, and where each team was running next. They asked some of us new guys what we thought about our first race and were sincere in their observations about how well we had run. There was an excitement and connection with this band of scraggly strangers that I had never felt before in competitive sports.

If you were 18 years old in 1972, your future included a draft number or some expensive Vietnam aversion tactic

26

that most people from my part of the world were probably not going to be able to afford. The last year of high school for many of these runners was probably a year of fears and uncertainty that I was too young to understand at 14. I am sure that being around young men who could laugh and encourage, finding a way to focus their attentions on something other than the troubles of the world has flavored the way I feel about running. Being able to rise above the daily struggles and compete in a sport requiring dedication and the ability to concentrate fully for long periods of time is something admirable.

Being able to do it with a smile is the main lesson I learned early.

Steve Adkisson finishing at home course 1972.
Spectator Yearbook photo

JUGGERNAUTS

"One cannot consent to creep
when one feels the impulse to soar."

-Helen Keller (1880-1968)

The next day at school the principal read out our names and places from the meet. Coach had given him the results of the meet earlier that morning. The principal told Coach that the Morning Announcements had never included results from the cross-country team. But Coach said, "That's funny. Monday I could've sworn I heard you talk for five minutes about the football game from Friday night, including who scored, who lead the team in tackles, their perfect 1 and 0 record, who they were playing this week, and . . ."

"Ok, ok," the principal said. "I got it."

"Just equal treatment for these kids. That's all I want." Coach said.

I knew this conversation had occurred because a girl in my homeroom told me. She was getting an early dismissal signed when coach walked in and handed the principal the results. She said the principal was not real happy about it, but he did it as asked and continued to do it after every meet for the entire season.

The result of this was that after a few weeks, people started asking about the meets. I thought it was pretty cool to hear our names called out and it definitely upped the ante for each of us to do a little better each time out. Coach was a master at using peer pressure to accomplish a difficult job. Everybody knows self-motivation is the best motivation, but it helps if the whole world knows what the results were.

I had made a new friend, Alice, who was also a freshman and who volunteered to write for the weekly school

29

newspaper The Tatler. She had asked me some questions about running in the first couple of weeks of school after hearing the announcements and submitted her first story to the paper about the cross country team:

Go Ask Alice
Lloyd CC Team

-The Tatler, Volume I 1972

"This year's cross-country team is coached by Mr. Daley. He has coached at Talbert City, KY. and Dexter, Missouri where he coached football, cross-country, and track. When the team isn't running, they are over at the Middle School playing other sports. He also has kids from the seventh and eighth grades in training, some run reserve. They are: Roger Black, Connie Easton, Doug Reed, Keith Goodpaster, and Steve Morgan. The team managers are Matt Williams, Jeff Ogden, and Gary Eades. The other members of the team are Kevin Moore, Bill Comley, Dean Herron, and Gary Graves. Doug Roberts is a junior. Sophomores are Matt Huff, Mark Roberts, Roy Murr, Steve Nienaber, and Greg Maston. Freshman: Steve Adkisson, Terry Brake, Herald Hensley.

Steve said that he runs because he likes it, and plans to break a school record and run his remaining years at Lloyd, also.

Mark Roberts felt that he ran hard at first, but they had to get in shape fast."

Alice was proud of her first published article, and I was equally thrilled to see my name in print for the first time.

Over the next few years she would hone her writing skills into a psychedelic style that created a great interest in the paper – just to see what she was going to come up with next. She wrote about anything and everything but nearly always had an article in each issue about the cross-country team during the fall.

Over the next several months of training, we worked extremely hard in practice. Our total mileage wasn't high by comparison to what we would do in later years, but the intensity of our interval workouts was very high. I did not really have language to describe in my log book the difficulty of some of the workouts, and the simple description of "hard" must have meant a particularly painful day.

The rest of my freshman season was full of hard lessons. We trained every day and I learned the things every new runner has to learn, and mostly I learned them the hard way, many of them twice: Your feet get blisters if you decide to do a long run in brand new shoes without breaking them in. You're likely to throw up if you eat too soon before you run, or you eat or drink the wrong things too soon before you run. Sprinting out to the lead in a long race feels great, but it really stinks when all those guys you sprinted by come filing by you a half mile later. Staying up late to listen to the Reds play the Dodgers on the West Coast is fun, but getting up at 6:00 the next morning to get on the team bus to Louisville isn't.

As I put these lessons into practice, I found I was hanging on to the lead group for longer and longer in our races. I managed to be our number three runner consistently and our entire team was showing signs of strengthening as the season went along. Gary said that in the four years he'd run the team had been dead last or next to last in the regional meet. We managed to win several dual meets, so we knew we were better than at least a few of the teams we would be

31

competing against.

There was also a new sense of team spirit growing amongst the members of the team. We got together to watch the TV broadcast of the Floyd Patterson vs. Mohammed Ali fight at Madison Square Gardens. Being a Wednesday night, this was the first time my parents had let me stay out late on a school night and I took that as a vote of trust on their part that being a member of this team was something they approved of. Not that they didn't trust me or the people involved, but running was something new to all of us, and I am sure they had the same fears all parents have about the changes their kids are going to go through. I had been something of a xenophobe up to this time, and they probably looked at my venturing out as a positive experience.

Hanging out with my older teammates was every bit the learning experience that school was. They talked about the news of the world, like the war in Vietnam, Richard Nixon, and the Israeli invasion of Lebanon, and how this was related to the terrorist killing and kidnapping at the Munich Olympics. I was amazed at how intelligent and aware many of them were.

Matt Huff qualified to compete in the Kentucky High School Cross-Country State Championship by finishing in the top five in our Regional Championship. Our team was disappointed to finish fourth, but considering that our school had been a perennial bottom dweller, we viewed our season a complete success. Matt was easily our best runner and as a sophomore still had great potential to improve before he graduated.

I felt honored when Coach asked me along with a couple of others to continue training with Matt the week between the Regional and State meets. Many of my teammates were trying out for basketball and I was also planning to tryout, but Coach said I was excused from the first week of tryouts if I was still actively participating in a fall sport. He had arranged it with the basketball coach.

Since my one and only cross country season consisted of running in the beautiful Kentucky fall months of August, September, and October, I was almost sorry I had been asked to run when we went out on this last Monday in October to find cold, blowing rain mixed with sleet. The running gear I owned consisted of a pair of gray sweatpants with a waist tightened by a shoestring, a navy zippered sweatshirt with the zipper stuck about half way down, a stocking cap, and a pair of cotton gloves. Ten minutes into an 8-mile run, I was completely soaked and questioning myself why I was out here.

We ran three abreast out the country road where there was little or no traffic, not saying much.

"I bet them pansies from Owensboro are sitting in the whirlpool," Gary finally said.

Matt gave this a minute to sink in, and then added: "I bet we could win the Region next year."

Gary was the only one of us that day who would graduate before next cross-country season and the rest of us were just freshman and sophomores. Matt was hoping to place in the top ten at State and the rest of us had gradually closed the distance between ourselves and him to the point where we could see ourselves closing a lot of that distance with another year of training.

"If you all keep running, you could probably win State in a couple of years," Gary suggested.

The idea of being a State Champion had not really sunk in to me. I did not have any real aspirations when the season started and was just now beginning to get a sense of the seriousness that runners attach to accomplishing a feat like winning a Regional or State Championship. Our team had performed well in the Region and even I could understand that just cutting fifteen or twenty seconds from our 2-mile times would make a big difference in our finishing places. If just a few of us had beaten a couple more of our competitors at the Regional, our team would have finished well enough for us to have qualified to compete in the State Meet.

That rainy Monday run turned out to be the worst day of the week since Coach knew how to taper his runners really well. We had peaked at the Region running our best races of the year on the right day. Matt's training was pretty much over so the most important thing for him this week was to rest and be mentally prepared to give another strong effort at the State Meet.

After school Friday, we loaded in to Coach's car and traveled down to Richmond, Kentucky where we would stay with the grandparents of Coach's wife, Becky. Doc Houston was the resident physician at Eastern Kentucky University. The State Meet was held at a nearby park and Coach Daley had arranged for us to spend the night at Doc and Mrs. Houston's antebellum house.

Aside from being the largest house I had ever stepped foot in, I was wide-eyed just to be along for this great adventure. My family camped and visited relatives, but we rarely traveled so any trip was almost an odyssey to me. Dr. and Mrs. Houston were fantastic hosts and made us feel important for our running accomplishments. Their easy going manner belied the important contributions they had made to the rural community around Boone County. I would learn later when I worked on Doc Houston's farm that he was an auspicious physician in Northern Kentucky, having been one of just a handful of area doctors after World War II. He delivered more babies and fixed more busted up farmers than any other doctor of his era. He had been stationed in Germany late in the war and had a room in his barn full of boxes of German plunder which included medical equipment along with Nazi weapons he brought back from the war.

His humor and wit kept us entertained throughout the evening before the meet and I was excited for Matt when we finally lay down to go to sleep. It was difficult getting my eyes to close with all the anticipation of what the next day would hold. I had never seen a meet with 300 runners and knowing it included only the best teams from each region made me want to do whatever it took to get our whole team back here for next year's meet.

Even my imagination could not have prepared me for the real thing. When we drove into the parking lot the next day, I was amazed at all the people who had traveled to see the State Championship. At our biggest meet, the Regional Championship, there were maybe 100 spectators, mostly parents, girlfriends, brothers and sisters of the runners. At our home meets after school, the spectators may have numbered twenty.

Around the parking lot here were over fifty school buses. There were some school pep bands set up and playing their school's fight songs, concession stands selling coffee and donuts to the early morning spectators, and people milling around their team's runners wearing the letter jackets and sweaters of a hundred different Kentucky High Schools. It was the most colorful and exciting sporting event I had ever seen.

Matt did his warm-up out on the course by himself and with about ten minutes to go before his race was due to start, he came over to where we were standing with Coach.

Coach gave him some last minute tactical advice about not getting boxed in early. Matt was very fast and had great competitive instincts so Coach new if he was up at the front of the pack, he would stand a good chance of hanging with the leaders.

We joined Matt in a mini-huddle. He had that bellicose look in his eyes that I would witness on many occasions in the future. It scared me to see it in a face that was almost angelic at any time other than when he was preparing himself for a race. We were as nervous as he was psyched, even though he was the only one actually running.

I had asked Matt the night before how you get ready for something like the State Meet. Matt was an outstanding swimmer and had competed in age group swimming since he was five. He had competed in many huge swimming events and he told me that he applied the same philosophy to running as he did with swimming.

"My swim coach always told us to trust our training," he said. "If you've done the work to get yourself ready, you will see the results on race day. But at a certain point, all you can do is pray."

We put our hands together and recited the Lord's Prayer and then Gary said "Juggs, on three" and counted.

We shouted "Juggs!" and Matt jogged back to the starting line while we sprinted off to the side to get a good view of the start.

When the starter's pistol fired and the huge pack of runners went sprinting out, I was almost sad I wasn't out there flying over the wet grass covered with the falling leaves of late autumn.

The course wound around the park and several of us sprinted through a short stretch of woods to get another view of the runners as they passed by. Matt was in the top fifteen when they came by about 800 yards into the race. I could tell he was going at full speed, but he had a determined look on his face and was not showing any signs of slowing down.

Just five or six minutes later, the front of the pack came into view on the horizon sprinting for the finish line. They had about 600 yards to go when we first saw them and the race at the front was a dogfight between three runners. Two of them were from the same school and wore blue and white, while the other wore the red and white striped Owensboro High School uniform that I would come to be very familiar with. All three of them finished within a stride of each other and the impression left on me was that the Owensboro runner just wanted it more than the others. They all looked like they were staggering from their 2 miles of maximum exertion and it came down to who wanted it the most in the last 10 steps. I always remembered the faces of those three as they were finishing and the only face that changed from a contorted grimace to an exultant smile was the face of the winner.

Matt finished a very strong 12th in his first State Meet and we were all very proud of his accomplishment. He seemed a little disappointed at first, but on the way home Coach told him that this was the first State Meet in history where fifteen runners had run the two mile faster than ten minutes. The whole field was getting faster as the sport of running was gaining momentum throughout the state.

Bishop Brossart High School, the team that we lost to in our first meet of the season, captured the small school State Championship. We watched their race and witnessed the excitement of their hard earned victory. The fact that I had come so far in the few months since we raced them, and knowing that they were kids much like us, gave me a way of realizing something like that was possible.

I sat quietly and looked out the window for most of the two hour drive home. I was truly saddened by the thought that the season was over, but I was already thinking about how I would get prepared to come back for next year's meet. About half way home it started to rain. The mood of everyone in the car became subdued. I think all the wheels were grinding toward the same destination, and everybody had their individual ruminations to deal with. I was thinking "Get fast . . . Get fast . . ."

Later that evening I sat in our bedroom making notes in my logbook. I wrote down some things I wanted to remember for next year and went back and read through each day's entry from the first day of practice. The log for this first year is unremarkable in most respects except one: the daily entries confirm that I did not take a single day off from running from the first day of school until the day before the State Meet when I took a "rest" day.

JUGGERNAUTS

"If this life be not a real fight, in which something is eternally gained for the universe by success, it is not better than a game of private theatricals from which one may withdraw at will. But it feels like a real fight, as if there were something really wild in the universe which we, with all our idealities and faithfulnesses, are needed to redeem."

-William James (1842-1910)

The Monday after watching my first State Cross-Country Championship was the day the basketball coaches made the first cut of the tryout period. I had been excused from the previous week so they couldn't cut me on my first day. I got to stay for the rest of the tryout period and even though I was a little rusty, I managed to make some shots and play good enough defense to show the coaches I was worth keeping around. I made the freshman team and got to play a fair amount.

I started playing basketball in the Catholic Youth League in 3rd grade and had played every year since then. Even considering my size I was pretty good. I was always one of the starting five players on the team I played on and was an even better street ball player where all of us had learned to play a style of basketball where fouls were rarely called and you had to learn to finish with the ball going into the basket. I fancied myself a cross between Pistol Pete Maravich and Earl Monroe. In my neighborhood, as well as nearly every Kentucky community, it was almost a violation of the building code for your driveway not to have a permanently installed backboard and rim.

As much as I love to play basketball, I hated watching from the sidelines for even a few minutes. After one season of cross-country I had already learned there was a sport that didn't have halftimes, dugouts, sidelines, or substitutions. When the basketball season was coming to an end, I was already getting antsy to get back to a sport without a bench.

Those of us who had run cross-country talked all winter about which events we wanted to run once the track season began. Some of the experienced guys would talk about their times and how much they were expecting to improve. I had no idea what kind of times I would run, but I knew I could keep up with several of my teammates who had respectable 880, mile, and 2-mile times.

By the time the track season was over, I had run a 4:55 mile as well as winning some points for the varsity track team in the 880, mile, and 2-mile. The track racing was a whole new competitive experience for me. Cross-country was one race for everybody and the team aspect was something that motivated me more than the "points" you earned for your team in a track race. In cross-country, if you had five or more good distance runners, you could do extremely well. But in track, you could have just two or three really good runners and win the meet if those athletes ran every distance event. I had a hard time feeling connected with the shot putters, long jumpers, and hurdlers even though they were my teammates. The races I ran were definitely suited to me: the 880, the mile, and the 2-mile. It was still distance running but each race had its own distinct physical requirements. I was able to do pretty well at it because, even as a kid, I had participated in a great variety of endurance sports without really knowing what I was doing.

History will most likely dispute it. The record books will never document it. Few will believe it, but I was actually there the day the sport of Triathlon was invented. I can not pinpoint the date, but me, my older brother Billy, my cousin Mark, and my little brother John were all there that summer day in 1969.

JUGGERNAUTS

I come from a large family and an even larger extended family of uncles, aunts, cousins, and grandparents. Our families often went together on fishing and camping trips. The men would kick back over some beers and do some serious fishing. Our moms would look after all the little kids and catch up on the various local gossip. The boys would wander off into the woods or down the shore of the lake and catch fish, crawdads, and any other creature that had the misfortune to wander into our range.

The fish were not biting particularly well this day and it was hot, too hot to fish. In Kentucky, you know it's too hot to fish when the worms look like they're working up a sweat when you bring them up for the air you believe they need every three minutes. One thing I've never understood about fishing is how it can be considered so much fun when you don't actually catch any fish. I love to be outdoors. I love serenity. I love to admire nature's beauty. But when I put a lure or live bait on a hook, I expect to get a nibble every once in a while. There was no such thing as catch-and-release fishing where I came from. If we caught it, it was going to be eaten.

After about a half hour of fishless fishing, our young minds took to exploring the shore line and it didn't take long for Johnny to discover a rusted out bike that somebody must have stashed in the woods and forgot to come back for. We figured this out by counting the layers of leaves that covered the back tire and wheel. After a few minor adjustments such as putting on the chain and duct taping the handlebars in a more or less upright position, we pulled the bike up the slope from the lake. We'd sent my youngest brother Wayne, whose nickname at the time was Chongo, back to the campsite to fetch the air pump, and when he returned we were able to inflate the tires with only a slight constant hissing coming from each one.

Billy, being the oldest and biggest, decided he got to ride it first. I had already decided I would wait my turn when I noticed that this bike seemed to have a freewheel action and a coaster brake. I was not much of a bike mechanic at the time, but I had a feeling something wasn't exactly right with this setup.

The shore was only about a hundred feet and 45 degrees below where we had managed to get the bike. Billy set the front wheel downhill and was about to holler "Get out of my way" when he realized he should be hollering "May Day May Day". It only took about three seconds from launch to dismount, but in those three seconds I thought at least ten things: "Oh man. Hold on. Watch out! How deep is that water? Pull out! Pull out! That *had* to hurt. Can I go next?"

The bike had several nifty features for an abandoned 1960's vintage Sears & Roebuck model. One of these was not a flotation system. Lucky for us, where Billy went face first into the water it was only about five feet deep and we waded in and got it out.

My cousin Mark was the next biggest and older than me, so he got to pull the bike up the hill and take his turn next. While Billy pulled the lake weeds out of his hair and emptied the contents of his pockets into his tackle box, Mark came back down the hill with a three-foot long piece of plywood he'd found on the hillside. He rolled a piece of a one-foot diameter log into the path and placed the plywood in front of it at about a 60-degree angle.

When he was satisfied the ramp would hold, he climbed the hill and mounted the bike. Now Mark had a reputation even at age twelve for being fearless. I'd seen him do some pretty hairy things with fish, like pretending a crappie was a bugle. He'd ridden his first steer calf when he was ten. Heights didn't scare him. But there was something about the way he sat up there and licked his lips that told me he had something worrying him about whatever it was he had in mind to do.

Maybe it was inertia that made the big heavy bike pick up more speed than he anticipated. Maybe it was the steepness of the hill he had underestimated. Maybe the angle of the ramp was more than he'd counted on.

Whatever the reason, when he got to the ramp he was easily going thirty miles an hour. His front tire hit the ramp and I could see the wood flex a little before it straightened out shooting the front end of the bike upward. I don't think the back tire ever touched the ramp because before it had a chance the whole rig was airborne.

I'll never know exactly what went through Mark's mind, but whatever it was told him to hang on for dear life. As the bike gained altitude and started through the first gainer, he glanced first skyward and then straight back at the three of us standing on the shore. His eyes were as big around as baseballs and I swear that what I saw was a smile on his upside down face as he reached the apex of his flight. He completed a second and slower gainer with his hands glued to the handlebars and his feet pedaling at ninety revolutions per minute as he floated through the equinox of his fall. If he had had another ten feet of descent he might have landed on top of the bike. He only had about five.

After a half-hour of diving to retrieve the bike and another half-hour of necessary repairs, it was my turn. In the time since Mark's trick, we had noticed there was a No Wake buoy about another 100 feet out from where he had landed. Since there was an intense sibling rivalry and considerable competitive spirit between all of us, it was agreed that what we would do was see who could jump the ramp, swim to the buoy and back, and run back up the hill the fastest. We hadn't thought of a name for the sport yet, but the foundation of bike, swim, and run was laid in this first event. Billy had one of those new fancy Zodiac Sea Wolf watches with a glow in the dark second hand and a swiveling bezel, so he would time each of us as we raced through the course.

Since it was my idea and finally my turn to ride, I got to go first. This ultimately turned out to be a crucial tactical decision made by shear instinct because not only had I inadvertently invented a new sport, I was the first winner in this first event. Being some thirty pounds lighter and seven inches shorter than either Billy or Mark, the Big Surfer (as we'd named the bike) turned out to be a little more than I could handle.

About half way down the grade, I knew I was in trouble. The line wasn't right.

There was not enough time to adjust and no brakes to slow the Big Goofy Bike (as I suddenly renamed it). Just as I could tell the front wheel wasn't going to hit the ramp but was instead aimed at the piece of log to the side of it, I jerked up on the handlebars in an attempt to lift the wheel. My idea was to position it to at least only hit the top half of the log instead of taking it straight on.

People have always said that I'm stronger than I look and this is one of those instances some people refer to when they make that statement. What happened then was one of the most spectacular unmanned bike wrecks ever witnessed. As I jerked upwards on the handle bars, the gooseneck came out of the collar at the same time that the front tire made contact with the log. The Big Stinky Freight Train Without A Track slowed enough that the speed of my body left it far behind. I was bounced out and flipped over the water with the handlebars out in front of me like a very competent divining rod. The Big Goofy Brakeless Bull

Without Horns did a picture perfect Endo and the rear wheel caught the edge of shore for another bounce before it splashed in behind me.

I had the competitive fire to drop the handlebars and swim for the buoy while the others dove in for the Fat Stinking Anchor With Spokes. I did a breast stroke turn around the buoy and freestyled it back to the shore. I squished through the muck and up onto the shore. I sprinted up the hill to the start/finish line and turned around to see the other three swimming back.

Billy hadn't gotten my time, but it really didn't matter. Mine turned out to be the only complete run of the course that day. Without handle bars, the Ol' Black Beauty which had taken me to this new world record would spend the rest of her days at the bottom of a cove in the Nolin River Reservoir.

Someday, I like to think, treasure hunters will go on an expedition to discover the mysterious sunken treasure of this first Triathlon Bike, which they would probably name the Predecessor Of Polycarbon Clipless Pedaled Boomerang Aerodynamic Pain In The Butt.

II
SOPHOMORE

"I know of no more encouraging fact than the unquestionable ability of man to elevate his life by a conscious endeavor."

-Henry David Thoreau

Even before the track season ended, I was already playing baseball on the same team I had played for in the previous three seasons. Between the daily track practices and baseball practice a couple times a week, I was having a great time. My friend Jude played baseball on the same team and we talked a lot about cross-country as we sat in the dugout between innings. He seemed real interested and I knew he was fast since we had raced up and down the halls in second grade and played baseball on the same team for eight years. When the third out was made and we were both in the outfield, we would race each other in to the dugout. He was always one of our best base stealers and covered a lot of ground playing centerfield. I kept bringing up the subject of him coming out to run cross-country with us and I guess I got through to him. When the baseball season ended, we started running together in the mornings before we went to work.

Jude had the perfect build for a distance runner. He was several inches taller than me and had a lean, muscular body. He ran with an effortless gait that made him look like he wasn't even really trying to run fast.

My brother John was getting ready for his freshman football season so he wanted to get ready for all the running he would have to do at football practice. He came along with us about half the time. He didn't have any trouble keeping up with us on these July morning runs and if he wasn't so determined to play football, I think I would have worked on him a little more to come out with us for cross-country.

Since I had a full year of training under my belt, I was beginning to understand the relationship between the volume of training you did and the speed you could hold over a longer distance. My log entries show a full summer of training which included some regular speedwork:

July 9 Intervals: 110, 220, 330, 440, 880, mile, 880, 440, 330, 220, 110 jog equal distance as rest Wt 97 total miles 4 avg 4

July 10 5 miles rest 10 minutes 5 miles ¾ effortWt 99 total miles 14 avg 7

July 11 Morning 5 miles Evening 5 miles feel sickWt 97 total miles 24 avg 8

July 12 No running – had important baseball gameWt 99 total miles 24 avg 6

July 13 1 mile on track in 5:32 330's 54, 51, 51,54, walk 110 Total 3 Wt 98 total miles 27 avg 5

July 14 No running – baseball game Wt 98 total miles 27 avg 4

July 15 Start Jr. Olympics training – 1 hour continuous run 8 miles Wt 96 total miles 35 avg 5

Jude caught on quickly and the two of us were really excited when the first day of cross-country practice finally arrived. Coach had announced at the end of the previous school year that we could begin practice on August 1st. Almost everyone who had run the previous season was coming back except for the two who had graduated. Coach Daley, being a Junior High Physical Education teacher, had recruited a bunch of Junior High kids to come out. There were a total of about twenty runners who showed up for the first team meeting.

On the first day of practice for my sophomore season, Coach gave us a more elaborate version of the short speech he had delivered the previous year. It was addressed more to the newcomers than to those of us who had experienced a year of cross-country under Coach's mentoring. After a brief introduction of all the runners, Coach began by laying out his simple rules:

"Be here on time. We start practice ten minutes after school lets out. You stretch out on your own. We're hardly ever here longer than an hour. You guys with cars, no peeling rubber in the parking lot. When practice is over you leave. I don't wait around here for your ride to pick you up. There's nowhere in this town that's too far to walk home. Don't let me catch you hanging around the school."

"You all might have heard somewhere that there's no such thing as a stupid question?" Coach paused here and waited for the inevitable hand to rise as several of the newcomers assumed that now was the time to ask.

"That's bullcrap," Coach said. "If you listen and pay attention, there shouldn't be any questions." Coach always held our meetings standing up. They didn't last that long.

He walked over to where he had laid his clipboard and picked it up. After glancing at it, he said that the only thing we were going to do today was get our physicals and do a short time trial.

Dr. Houston arrived a few minutes later to give us the Athletic Physicals required by the state to compete in a school sport. I entered these details in my Logbook: "August 1st – took physical 5'2 ½" 98 lbs. bp 105/58 hr 54 Run 1320 – 3:59 5 x bleachers".

The second day of practice was when it started to get interesting.

Coach had us run five miles to a turn-around marker out the country road heading west from the school. It started out as a normal steady run but as we got to the turn-around, the pace heated up to pretty much of an all-out race coming back. I wasn't sure what got it started, but there were four or five of us hammering along when we got about a half-mile from the school. I think Matt wanted to show us all that he was still the man to be reckoned with, but I also knew I was a lot stronger than the previous year. Jude just thought this was what cross-country practice must be like since it was his first day of real practice. He was cruising along with us until he faded a little near the very end. Steve Nienaber was another Junior who had come back after running the previous year. He was an age group swimmer along with Matt. He was obviously in pretty good shape from the summer of competitive swimming and he hung on to the fast pace all the way through the end.

I don't know exactly when I realized it, but it was in the very early days of this season that I started becoming aware there was something special about the group of people who were there running beside me. It is hard to put your finger on the reason behind this uniqueness, but it probably has something to do with the blending of diverse personalities with a common goal. We never talked about it, but everyone had a different reason for being out there. We all knew that the effort we were putting out in training would eventually lead us to something we all wanted, even if that something wasn't clearly defined. There was still very little fame or notoriety associated with running so it wasn't for the glory of it because there was none.

I was only fifteen so I didn't think about it all that much, but whatever was going on kept me excited about getting up in the morning to go out and train. I found myself really looking forward to going out for a 5-mile morning run before getting to my chores or heading off to work. My older brother Bill had helped get me a job as a busboy at the Holiday Inn where he worked. Early in the summer I worked 3 – 11, so sometimes I would run after I got off work too. When cross-country practice started, I was able to change my work schedule to 7 a.m. to 3 p.m. and we would run before work and then again in the evening with the team.

With all the running I did that summer, I couldn't help but improve. My Logbook entry for August 5, 1973 notes my first ever Tape Breaking: *"Jr. Olympic Under 16 Mile. Warm-up 30 minutes 1st with a 4:50.8 66,77,82, 65 I did it!"*

The only thing I remember about that race now is that it was on a cinder track and that I had a phenomenal kick. It's funny how the many important details of a race get blurred into a single image that sticks. Sometimes it is the people you were with; sometimes it is the competition, the weather, or the pain of the race. How I managed a 65 last lap after slowing to 82 is a complete mystery to me. The feeling of the cinders grinding under my spikes is the only lasting memory of accomplishing what my Logbook said was my one and only *"Goal for Summer - 1st in Jr. Olympic Mile"*.

". . . And Jim said you mustn't count the things you are going to cook for dinner, because that would bring bad luck. The same if you shook the tablecloth after sundown. And he said if a man owned a beehive and that man died, the bees must be told about it before sunup next morning, or else the bees would all weaken down and quit work and die. Jim said bees wouldn't sting idiots; but I didn't believe that, because I had tried them lots of times myself, and they wouldn't sting me."

Huck Finn
Adventures of Huckleberry Finn
-Mark Twain

In the first week of September we had our first meet of the season. About ten minutes before the start of the race, a familiar white Comet roared into the parking lot and our teammate Gary from last year skidded his car into a parking spot just as we were finishing our last strideout. We jogged over to his car and leaned in the windows.

"Listen to this," he said and turned the volume up on the radio.

An acoustic guitar began to play and Matt asked, "What's up?"

"Oh, I just got off work and thought I'd see how the team was looking," Gary answered.

Leaning into the car from the passenger side, I could detect the distinct smell of chocolate. Gary worked in the Erlanger Chocolate Factory unloading truckloads of 100 pound bags of chocolate powder used to make chocolate syrup and the smell stayed on his clothes and in his car as long as he had that job.

The song continued to play: "There's a lady who's sure

all that glitters is gold and she's buying a stairway to heaven. When she gets there she knows if the stores are all closed with a word she can get what she came for."

We all stood around and listened to the song, which was pretty long for a radio station to play. Before it was over, Coach hollered to us to get ready.

Gary got out of his car and came out to join us in our traditional huddle. His presence there added a familiarity that all of us were glad to have. As the first race of a new season, the butterflies were spiraling around in my stomach and I think each of us was uplifted judging by the smiles and laughs when Gary told us another of his infinite repertoire of dirty jokes.

We said our prayer and paused a minute in a tight huddle with our hands joined in the center. "Bite Me on three," Gary instructed us. He had an impish grin on his face like he just couldn't wait to see the reaction to this. "Ready," he said and then counted "One, two, three. . ."

A muffled unintelligible sound erupted from the huddle as we all laughed at the mere thought of the trouble we would be in if we had carried out the huddle breaking cry that we had come close to executing. Later I told my mom we had shouted "Strike Three!" when she asked about it. Now that Gary was out of school, he didn't have to live with the consequences that would come from Coach if he misbehaved. I got a sense from last year that Coach and Gary did not exactly see eye to eye about some things. Their relationship had gotten off to a tempestuous start and went downhill from there. Gary had spent three years running for the previous coach and was slow to buy into the new paradigm of running that Coach Daley brought with him. To their credit, neither of them would badmouth the other. Coach even seemed happy to see Gary when we broke from the huddle and Gary went over to shake his hand.

Whether it was Gary's exorcising of the butterflies or just the simple fact that we were in much better shape than last year, we ran really well in the first meet. I finished second to Matt in 10:12 and our team scored just twenty-six points in a four-team race. Our top five runners ran faster times than we had the previous year and several new runners including Jude had been very impressive in their first race.

It didn't take long for the other schools to find out that we were a tough bunch of young runners. Coach also had us believing this ourselves and a metamorphosis had occurred over the summer due to our dedication to the daily training we did.

Coach Daley had a way of bringing out the toughness in everyone he coached. The workouts were all designed to get us accustomed to the kind of suffering that every runner experiences in racing. Maybe we were all predisposed to needing more suffering than the normal person needs, and in many ways that might have been true for some of us. But even the runners on the team who you might think were "soft" if you just hung out with them revealed an unexpected tenacity when they were out on a cross-country course.

The word "tough" was one Coach Daley used a lot. "These 440's will make you tough" or "These guys you're racing are all tough hill runners" were common statements. Our workouts for my second year were already a lot harder than anything we had done the previous year. Coach had scouted out several difficult challenges for us including something we called "Agony Steps."

There is a park overlooking the Ohio River in Northern Kentucky called Devou Park. One of the highest points in the area looks straight down at the towns of Covington and

Newport in Kentucky and Cincinnati just across the river. Someone, in one of the cruelest uses of concrete you could imagine, had built a set of steps that went basically from the river to the top of this overlook. The steps had fallen into disrepair over the years so several of them were catty-wampus or had sunk into the ground as the hillside slipped under the combined forces of gravity and erosion. The result of this was that those particular steps were quite a bit higher than the building code would call for, often a good thirty inches tall. We would do repeats of running up the steps and walking back down as the recovery between the repeats.

Each run up the steps would take us about four minutes on a good day, longer if you were tired or if you weren't in shape for this workout. It was probably less than half a mile in length but at about a 30 degree angle. When we reached the top, it was all we could do to keep our wobbly legs from buckling underneath us. Coach would never tell us how many repeats we were going to do beforehand. He may not have known himself until he saw how we were handling the workload, so we always ran as hard as possible thinking if we looked completely spent, or if more than one person puked, he would not send us down for another run up the steps. This didn't always work.

Coach knew how to bring the new runners along to make them want to improve. It was probably only a logical thing for him to do but one of the many clever incentives he used was to group the runners into three groups when we went out to run: Fast, Slow, and Beginner. Now I was never in anything but the "fast" group but I don't think there was a kid on the team who wanted to be in the "slow" group. Guess what? many of these runners found that they were capable of a lot more speed than they thought they had when they started.

Coach would say "I want the fast group to go all the way to the end of the road and then turn around, the slow group to go to the big tree at the end of Long's farm, and the beginners to go out to for 20 minutes and turn around." He knew that if everyone ran about the pace he thought they could run the whole team would finish at about the same time. You can imagine what happened.

The fast group would turn around and try to catch the slow group. The slow group would turn around and try to catch the beginners. And everybody would run hard to not get caught by the group coming up behind them. As the season went along, the fast group got bigger as Coach promoted those who had demonstrated they could do better.

Devious plan, but it made you tough.

School started out to be something of a drag. My brother Bill told me that sophomore year was the hardest and after a few weeks I was beginning to think maybe he was right. I can't quite put my hand on it, but somehow there was a greater expectation from the teachers about what we should have already known coming into our sophomore year. They were not bashful about telling us about it.

The biggest motivating force for me was the opportunity to be eligible for the "Straight A" tickets that the Cincinnati Reds organization offered. Any student who could present a report card that had all A grades would be given four free tickets to a game. Even though the season would be over by the time the first grading period came around this fall, I wanted to position myself to get in on this when spring rolled around. Several of my friends had earned them and I had attended at least fifteen games over the summer to see one of the greatest professional baseball teams of all time. The Reds were set up to be really good next year and I wanted to cash in on this opportunity to get free tickets.

My grades were decent for the entire Freshman year, but getting all A's was looking like a real challenge. When I had signed up for classes I thought I had a pretty decent schedule. I knew Algebra I would be hard, but I had no idea English II, Spanish I, Biology, and History would be as demanding as they were. I got into the Shop class I had missed out on in Freshman year and I really enjoyed it. Mr. Reynolds taught shop and was also my homeroom teacher. He had broken his arm before school started and wore a cast on his dominant right hand so he used a yardstick in his left hand to point things out to us. He was never reluctant to use this ruler to enforce a safety rule or make a point about discipline so I quickly became familiar with the business end of it. We started right in to woodworking and I was already pretty well familiar with table saws and lathes, so I was often used to demonstrate some of the basics since Mr. Reynolds was not able to use both of his hands and safely show the class how to do some of the procedures required to operate the tools.

Algebra just doesn't make sense to me. I know it is supposed to be a discipline which teaches problem solving skills on a much deeper level than simple equations presented in the textbooks, but somehow the concept of x's and y's being interpolated for reasons only the teacher knows just always seemed like a form of meaningless torture for me. I did well for the first few weeks, but as the problems grew more and more abstract, I grew frustrated with the reasoning that this was somehow important to my future. I started having to take my book home and knew I was in trouble when I started asking my sister in 8th grade to help me with my homework, and she could.

English II was mostly diagramming sentences and I

could not get beyond the idea that if I could read the sentence and understand its meaning that I needed to know about and be able to identify the prepositions, antecedents, past or future tense, or the difference between nouns, verbs, and adverbs. I knew I was in trouble when a question on the first quiz of the year included the question: "True of False: Abrogates is the third person singular simple present indicative form of abrogate." Somehow I figured the English language would survive without my personal intimacy with the specific participles involved in producing written versions of it. My teacher thought otherwise.

Spanish was something completely foreign to me, but I had a great memory for the vocabulary and found it much easier than trying to learn English as it was taught in the classroom. My Spanish teacher was among the best teachers in the school and it was evident how much she loved teaching by how well she did it. Each week we increased the number of Spanish words in our vocabulary and gradually were becoming familiar with the grammar and usage of common phrases, but it took a lot of repetition for me to get it right. I practiced at home with my younger brothers and sisters. They learned it as quickly as I did.

Biology was interesting but I got lost immediately when taxonomy switched to Latin. I found it extremely annoying that somebody thought a muskie should be called *essox muscilungi,* or a wolf should really be called *canis lupis.* I could not get it through my thick skull that there had to be two names for everything under the sun, nor that there would be a test on it at the end of the week.

Early on, we started studying cells and there was so much new information being discovered that sometimes the day's newspaper contradicted the textbook. The cell terminology was always a challenge too, because even pronouncing "mitochondria," "gamete," and "nucleus" was difficult. I worked hard at remembering the terms and definitions long enough for the quizzes. Much beyond that was too much to expect.

My History class was taught by Mr. Partin who was at least eighty years old and could have retired twenty years before. He would give a reading assignment to the class and sit at his desk reading the paper until he fell asleep. He worked at night at the horse track and since he had tenure and nothing to lose for doing a poor job of teaching he didn't really care. We had two tests each quarter covering the reading assignments and the tests were a lot harder than I expected since he never lectured or gave any hint about what would be on them.

The Kentucky High School Athletic Association had guidelines for academic eligibility for athletes to compete and Coach Daley had yet another higher standard. He knew all the teachers and would be the first one to get on us if something was slipping at school. My parents expected me to do the best I was capable of doing and so I strived to do well at each of these classes even though I found it difficult to really give my full energy to school when my mind was always on running.

STEVE ADKISSON

"The will to win means nothing without the
will to prepare."

-Juma Ikangaa,
Tanzanian 2:08 marathoner

Our season had gone along with a steady stream of
close races. I won't say we were superstitious but we developed a certain amount of necessary routine and a fairly
regimented pre-race ritual. Since most of the better runners
on the team were also swimmers, many of them wore
Speedos under the school issued team shorts. I had bought
a pair even though I was not much of swimmer because the
Speedos were a great replacement for the traditional jock
strap and they could be washed easily in the shower and be
ready to go again the next day. They quickly became my
"lucky" Speedos and after a while most of us just kept them
on all the time except when they were drying overnight on
the towel rack in the bathroom.

We had made a tape of the Led Zeppelin song that we
heard on Gary's radio before our first race of the season,
"Stairway to Heaven," and we always managed to get to
somebody's car in the half hour before a race started to
play the tape. As we listened to it, our moods would become more serious. When the song was over, we would
head out for a long warm-up run, and then spend a few
minutes stretching before putting on our spikes and running
a set of 8 times 100 yard stride outs.

We always huddled up where we stopped after our last
100 stride out so we were somewhat distant from the
coaches and spectators when we prayed and had Gary deliver a new joke. We never used the same 'huddle break
phrase' but some of the more memorable ones would not be

printable in anything less than an R rated version of this text. The only thing that saved us from the wrath of Coach or our parents was that we were far enough away and usually laughing too hard for the words to be clear and audible

We were third in our first big race, the Covington Catholic Invitational and I was 12th place individually. We lost by one point in a dual meet to the Highlands Bluebirds who had won the Regional Championship the year before. We won several dual meets and were competitive even in the meets we lost against most of the other teams of our region. I was consistently our number two runner.

Coach held Matt out of a race in late September when he had a cold as well as some soreness in his foot. It was a three-team meet, which we called Triangular Meets. I took advantage of this opportunity to race against a field that did not include the best runner in the region by winning my first cross-country meet. *"Sept 27 – Meet LMHS, SK, Beechwood – We won! 1st 10:11 (4:58 first mile) Matt didn't run - sick"* was how I noted this in my log.

There is something about breaking the tape that can not be understood until you've done it. It is like the feeling I imagine musicians have the first time they play a piece of music in front of a large audience and the audience responds with a loud applause. "Applause junkies" is how the entertainment industry refers to it, but with endurance athletes it is much the same. The feeling of being the first to finish and knowing it took everything you had to do it is something you want to have happen again. It is addictive in the sense that it will make you do strange things to obtain that feeling over and over again. Things like setting an alarm clock at 5:15 a.m. on a school day, put on three layers of cotton sweat pants to go out for a run in a blizzard, go to bed at 9:00 on a Friday night so you'd be rested for the Saturday morning race.

Our next three weeks of training were the hardest of the year. We ran a lot of dual meets during our season, usually on Tuesdays and Thursdays. In between we did long intervals like 8 x 880 in 2:40, or 20 x 440 at 75 seconds with one minute rest. We did a long run of twelve miles, and eight miles was a pretty normal afternoon run. Because our regional race was to be held on a particularly hilly course, Coach had us run twenty-five hill repeats on the hill in front of the school several times a week, usually after our long runs. I was getting pretty used to almost daily hard efforts even though there were supposed to be some easy days thrown in to the program. All of the varsity team was getting stronger and growing in confidence when the day of the Regional Meet came.

In early October, it rained hard enough to cancel a planned race, but we ran eight miles hard on hills in the some of the worst conditions I'd ever been out in. The next day, a Friday and the afternoon before our Homecoming Dance, we ran 8 x 880 on the "Trail of Tears" in front of the school. Over the weekend, we got together without Coach and did twelve miles easy on Saturday and ten on Sunday.

Lloyd Memorial High School had never won a regional cross-country championship in over thirty years of competition. Our biggest rivals, Highlands and Covington Catholic had beaten us in meets earlier in the season, but we were closing the gap and we realized we had a very strong team to go along with Matt's ability to win the Region individually.

On the day of the Regional Championship, a cold rain was blowing down on the course. The grass of the golf course was soggy and there were brown, orange, and red leaves carpeting most of the ground. As we warmed up, I noticed a grim resolve in all of my teammates. Our breath steamed out of our mouths as we jogged the one-mile course that we would have to race around twice.

We were not afraid of the competition. Each of us was fit and healthy. We were well prepared for the all-out whatever-it-takes effort to prove that, even though we were not considered contenders, our team had the best seven runners in northern Kentucky.

Some of the younger junior high kids often asked me what I do to get psyched up for a race. It has varied over the years, but it has never taken much to get me excited about trying to outrun a competitor. It must be something instinctive, something that is not even part of conscious thought, much like a thoroughbred racehorse. It is just their nature to run fast and try to run ahead of the other thoroughbreds. Darwin called it natural selection: the fastest one sends his genes on down the line. Just approaching a starting line and looking up and down the line at the other runners, measuring the amount of anxiety or confidence in their faces, and knowing how well prepared we were, was all it took to get us mentally ready for this race.

When they lined us up to start the race, I already knew we were going to win it. When we broke from the pre-race huddle, Matt had that look that said "just try to keep up with me" that I had seen now for a couple of seasons. Jude, Roy, Steve, Dave, Greg, and I fed off Matt's killer instinct and knew that if we ran as well as we were capable of running, Matt's one point as individual champion would keep our team score low enough to earn us the championship.

There was not a well-established 4, 5, 6, or 7 placer on our team as each of the runners who filled those positions would dog fight each other from race to race. The only thing Coach had emphasized in the weeks leading up to the Regional was that if our seventh man beat the other teams' fifth runners, there was no way we could lose.

This is one of the things I like best about the sport of cross-country: each runner from the fastest to the slowest can affect the outcome of a team race. If a team's slowest runner is faster than the other teams' slower runners, it makes a difference in the outcome.

What other sport is there where anyone but the superstars have such an impact on the results in the biggest competitions? Football teams often play only their best twelve or fifteen players in the games that matter the most, leaving the remaining twenty or thirty players to watch and cheer from the sidelines.

Most other team sports can be dominated by a couple of players. An outstanding pitcher in baseball can basically control the game, while a great shooter or ball handler can dictate the outcome of a basketball game.

Cross-country championships can be won without a great superstar (although it is nice to have one on your team!) The 1973 Lloyd Memorial High School Juggernauts, with Matt Huff as the individual winner, won the 9th Region Championship in Kentucky. Our team scored just 35 points to Highland's 60 as we earned our first trip to the Kentucky State Cross-Country Championship. I placed sixth individually, the first sophomore in the Region, which was something I tucked away as motivation for the future.

We weren't even supposed to be a serious contender in the Regional, so just placing in the top three would have been considered a victory. Winning was a surprise to everyone but the dozen or so of us who had trained hard for the previous four months. I don't doubt that our exuberance was visible but I do not ever remember anyone bragging about what we had done. We were proud of winning, but we knew that the Regional was just a big step toward the ultimate goal of winning a State Championship.

Matt Huff leads after 1st lap in 1973 Regional at Highland Country Club. Jude Baynum is running 7th, Steve Nienaber in Lloyd jersey just behind him. Author collection. Photographer not known.

Matt Huff winning 1973 Regional Race. Author collection. Photographer not known.

STEVE ADKISSON

Go Ask Alice
Lloyd Swifties Skip through Regional on Their Way to State

-The Tatler Volume VII, 1973

"In what may become an autumnal quotidian occurrence, the LMHS running Juggernauts made short work of their competition at the Regional Cross-Country Race held at Highland Country Club last Saturday. As the swirling orange and red maple leaves painted the air in helixes of descent, the blue and yellow clad Lloydsters wrought suffering – as much to themselves as to their adversaries. In their wake, they left rooster tails of plumed Highland Bluebird feathers. And if there is irony, and if there is such a thing as underdogism, our homeboys defined it.

Who besides the team, the coach, and their closest confidants would have given them a chance prior to Saturday's race?

In the first of what will be many firsts, the oligarchy of Coach Daley led by junior Matt Huff made the competition as feckless as Principal Fugate's Rambler at a drag strip. Matt as much as said "see ya" with a half mile to go, becoming an evanescent front runner as the others could not do much but wave goodbye.

Sophomore's Steve Adkisson and Jude Baynum followed close enough behind to smell the clutches burning and had a great view to watch the destruction. Juniors Steve Nienaber, Roy Murr, Greg Maston, and Dave Crump provided their yeoman's work to give the team a ticket to this weekend's State Meet in Louisville.

High fives to all the kinetic guys when you see them in the halls.

JUGGERNAUTS

On the Monday after the Regional, Coach decided to humble us a little bit by driving us to Devou Park for a last hard workout before we tapered for the State Meet. Devou Park has an amphitheater that sits in a natural earthen bowl. The stage at the bottom of the bowl is a couple of hundred feet below the lip, so Coach laid out a loop that started at the top, ran down and behind the stage, climbed to the opposite side, circled a tree before diving back down and then up to where the loop began. In the course of 400 yards, we climbed two long steep hills with two downhill sprints in between. Doing twenty-four repetitions of this loop was by far the hardest workout we had done all season. There were several runners on the team who had to walk the final uphill on the last several repeats. And these were runners who had run in the low 10:00's for two miles on a very challenging Regional course.

For the rest of the week, we just ran very easy for three or four miles each day. On the Friday afternoon before the State Meet, they held a combination football and cross-country pep rally on the football field. It was a little strange to me. Here we were doing our best to rest and conserve our energies for our biggest race ever while the cheerleaders and coaches took turns trying to rile us all up. The Principal delivered a soliloquy on excellence and ended it with an announcement that any student caught under the influence of alcohol at the football game that night would be suspended from school.

There is definitely a difference between what it takes to get a football team ready to take heads off their opponents and what is motivating to an endurance athlete. I know their intentions were good in recognizing us and presenting the Regional Champion trophy to us in front of the student body, but I was already preparing myself for the bigger race and I knew my teammates were also as psyched as

69

they would need to be to compete at their best.

As soon as the pep rally was over and school was dismissed, we loaded up in a couple of cars and headed to Louisville where the State Meet would be held the next morning. It was our first team overnight trip, and we were excited about the privilege of representing our school and our community. Coach repeated what many of our parents had told us as we left for school that morning that wherever we went, we were to mind our manners and behave in such a way as would bring honor to our team and our school. I personally had no idea what he was referring to since I had never known anyone on our team to be anything but polite, courteous, and respectful. I guess I was too young and innocent to know the kind of behaviors that coaches, parents, and administrator's fear from their student-athletes.

We drove straight to the racecourse and changed into our running clothes in the cars we had driven there. There were several other teams scattered around the course, which was marked with multi-colored flags and white lines. The course was almost pancake flat and the first half mile was a long straightaway that would require a lot of leg speed of any runner who wanted to be in contention when the race got serious in the last half. There were a few little roller coaster hills from the half-mile to one-mile points, and then the course circled back around reversing itself over the long flat section where it started.

We were very disappointed by how flat the course was since our training was based so much on making us good at the hilly courses we had to compete on in Northern Kentucky. We knew our greatest strength was our ability to run hills well, which didn't necessarily mean we had the speed necessary to race a flat two miles. Many of us had faster times on cross-country two-mile courses than we did in the two-mile on the track.

JUGGERNAUTS

I would never admit that we were beaten before we started but that's probably how it worked out. After a restless night of trying to sleep in a hotel room with three nervous teammates, I felt tired when we left the hotel for the course. Everybody seemed grim and somber, which might have been mistaken for being mentally focused if I didn't actually know better. None of us verbalized it, but just running over the flat hard grass surface the evening before had deflated us. We really didn't even know much about the competition, but we knew already that the terrain had neutralized our team's greatest strength. Once doubt enters a competitor's mind, it grows like a kudzu vine covering all the positive self talk with its thirty seven versions of "can't, won't, not, and no way".

We went through the motions of performing our prerace rituals, but I was as nervous as I had ever been before a sporting event. My hands were visibly shaking when we put our hands together to pray and I couldn't tell for sure, but it seemed like there was a common vibration not entirely caused by the tremors in just my hand. We jogged back to the starting line and all of us had our heads down and were glancing around at each other with what can only be described as "deer in the headlights" looks on our faces.

It was almost a foregone conclusion that none of us would perform well, given the complete lack of confidence and the utter absence of simply trusting our abilities to compete. When the gun went off, I felt like the entire field was speeding away from me, and as I went through the first half mile, I was running beside most of my teammates and many competitors who I had easily beaten throughout the season. My legs felt like I had lead weights around my ankles and it was a struggle just to keep going. The further along I went, the worse I felt. The worse I felt, the more I started belittling myself for my lack of effort. The more I beat myself up, the slower I ran until it was almost like I gave up completely near the middle of the race.

About a mile into the race, I started to pass a few people. As we came back around to where Coach was standing shouting encouragement, he hollered out "Come on Steve, you're better than that!" And he was right.

I could see several of my teammates up ahead and I pushed myself to catch up with them. We were placed well back in the field and there were several packs of what looked like entire teams grouped together ahead of us. We struggled through the back half of the course and finished looking respectably strong, but in reality we had come from so far back that it didn't help our team score very much.

The experts say that being a champion is seventy-five percent psychological and Yogi Berra added "the other half is mental." It took me a couple of years to fully learn this lesson, but the learning finally sunk in at the 1973 State Championship.

Our team finished 4th and I was 30th in 10:16. I had finished 6th in 10:03 in the Regional where I had beaten many runners who outperformed me in the biggest meet of the year. Most of my teammates had similar performances. Matt was our best performer and even he had finished further back than he had at last year's state meet.

The excitement of being Regional Champions was short lived. After the disappointing State Meet performance, we went into hibernation for a couple of weeks. My logbook reads:

"Sun Oct 29 Long Walk"
"Oct 30 – Nov 18 – Nothing – rest"

JUGGERNAUTS

We saw each other every day at school, but there was not the usual humor or enthusiasm that had been our normal way of interaction. There was no anger directed at the others, no blaming or making excuses. Each of us was hard enough on ourselves that there was no need for that. Coach, in fact, had seemed pleased with the outcome. Maybe he knew something we didn't, or maybe he just knew the relative importance of a cross-country meet, or any sporting event for that matter, in the overall scheme of things.

I guess it is pretty normal to be disappointed when you work towards a goal and don't accomplish it, or things turn out differently from what you wanted or expected. Time eventually heals all disappointments, so it was inevitable that we would get over it.

Only problem was, I am not sure some of us ever got over that feeling of hating to have our butts kicked.

1973 Team Photo
Spectator Yearbook photo.

1973 Regional Champions, 4th place in Kentucky State Championship. Back row: Greg Mason (on crutches), Dave Crump, Terry Brake, Steve Nienaber.
Front Row: Rick Murr, Jude Baynum,
Matt Huff, Steve Adkisson

By the end of November, things had settled back to normal. We developed a habit of getting together on Sunday afternoons to go hiking or somewhere out in the country away from town. There were several places which you could still consider wilderness and we would invariably end up somewhere near a lake or a creek and build a fire. My brother John, the Baynums, and several other friends - some runners and some not - were always up for an outdoor adventure. Aside from loving the outdoors, the other thing all of us had in common was being pyromaniacs. We were expert fire builders and could easily entertain ourselves for hours just tending and watching a fire.

I had read about the Finnish Olympic Champion runner Lasse Viren's use of the sauna as an enhancement to his overall health and fitness, so we would sometimes build up two or three fires and alternately sit in the heat between them and then plunge into the icy water.

It would have been a very strange site indeed for someone out hunting to come upon a half dozen winter whitened skinny kids come steaming out of the water in their boxer shorts and then squatting down on the gravel bank between three large bonfires.

We started running again in preparation for the spring track season and I joined up to be on the Swim Team at school. I had never been in competitive swimming, but several of my teammates had talked me in to trying it out. Coach Daley had offered to be the swim team coach in his first year and encouraged any of us who were interested to at least come to practice and use the YMCA pool as a workout. I figured I could get in some tough cardio workouts as a supplement to the running we were doing on our own.

We would end practice a lot of times with a half hour of water polo which is about as tough a workout as you could imagine, especially if you are not a great swimmer. Treading water and short intense sprinting to get to the ball or stop the other team from scoring is an incredibly challenging exercise.

Coach couldn't really work with us out of season due to some kind of Kentucky High School Athletic Association Rule, but he had offered to take us to a couple of races and this gave us something to look forward to. One of the races was the AAU Red Mile 10-Miler which was held literally on the Red Mile horse track at Lexington in early December. I had never raced farther than two miles, but we had done many training runs up to twelve miles, so I was confident I could go the distance.

Each lap of the track was one mile and we were given a time split each mile. I started conservatively since there were many college and open runners competing and they just took off. Realistically, I knew I did not have a chance to contend for a win. It was cold and the sand track was wet from rain the previous day but the footing was good. I found a pace that I thought I could maintain and made a challenge to myself to keep the mile splits as even as possible. I ended up finishing 24th in 1:03:53, which was respectable, but I realized near the end that I was not very well prepared for an hour of racing.

After the race and the drive home, I could hardly move my legs were so tired. The next day was even worse, but I made myself get out and run to loosen all the tight muscles up. As the next few days went by, the soreness gradually went away and I discovered the race had actually strengthened my system by tearing it down. I had new extra bounce in my step and had the confidence of knowing I could push myself much beyond what I had previously thought possible. This was a new key discovery for me: longer and faster runs build strength but you have to recover from the hard efforts to get the full effect.

Once New Year's came, we were rededicated to training for track and with the anticipation of bettering our times from last season, we were doing a lot of hard and fast interval training. Almost every day I would try to go into my highest gear at least for a part of my run. Most of our workouts were short, but very intense, almost races. In the evening I would run to my girlfriend's house which was exactly a mile from mine, and then end up nearly racing the mile home so I wouldn't miss my curfew of 10:00.

When March finally arrived and the official first day of

Track Season, I was in very good shape. Our first meet was on the 29th and I ran the mile in 4:43 and the 2-Mile in 10:26. My times hovered in this same range over the next month and it was frustrating not to see improvement, but I was patient and knew that doing two and sometimes three races in a meet was not the way to get the fastest times. I was training very hard between races and knew that when I rested and tapered, I would be able to make some break-throughs with my times.

In late April, we traveled to the Harrison County Invitational and I ran a 4:35.7 Mile but finished only 4th. This was my fastest time yet, and I was disappointed that I had not won. A few weeks later, I ran a 4:32.2, which was only good enough for 3rd place.

Finally, on May 11th at the Boone County Invitational, I was able to put in a good enough performance to win a race. It took place under what I found to be my favorite track race conditions. As the second to last event of the standard track meet schedule, the 2-mile usually takes place in the late afternoon or early evening. In this race, since there had been a lengthy rain delay earlier in the day, the sun had just set and the temperature had gone down from the high 70's into the low 60's. A very large crowd was on hand since this meet drew twenty or so teams from all around Kentucky, and there was a festive atmosphere as the teams were getting ready to pack up and end what had been a fun and exciting day of track and field.

When the rain started and the meet officials announced a delay, I went back to my house just a few miles away. Knowing my race would not start for several hours, I laid down and took a long nap. This was something that I had rarely done before a race, since most of our meets took place right after school or on a Saturday afternoon. When I woke up, I felt invigorated when I saw the weather had cleared up. I arrived back at the track just as they were re-starting the meet. I relaxed on the pole vault pits with my teammates and got up to encourage them when they went off to warm up for their races.

When the revised event schedule showed my race about thirty minutes away, I got my spikes out of my bag and held one in each hand while I jogged up and down the back straight for twenty minutes. Several of my competitors were making this same abbreviated circuit to avoid the commotion of the sprints taking place on the home straightaway. I didn't make conversation with any of them, but nodded to each one as we passed each other.

"Third call for the 2-mile" was announced over the speakers. I had done my stretching and put on my spikes just before the call came. I did several strides down the back straight before jogging clockwise around the turn headed for the starting line.

The track announcer introduced each runner and as each name was called, a few of the runner's teammates or friends would cheer. When my name was called, a loud cry went up from the pole vault pit, after which the announcer made the announcement that all athletes not competing should leave the infield immediately and join their teams in the bleachers.

We were called to the starting line and given the in-structions for the start.

The gun went off and I went right to the lead running comfortably at the goal pace I had set for myself of 75 sec-onds per lap. Several runners fell in right behind me and we cruised through the first mile at exactly 5:00. I was feeling very good and was encouraged by my teammates who had posted themselves at several different locations around the track.

The next few laps I picked up the pace and from the

way the crowd and my teammates were yelling, I thought there were several competitors right on my heels. I had already learned not to look back, but usually you have a sense about how close other runners are to you. Not being accustomed to leading, I was convinced I had to run harder to break away so I continued to push the pace faster.

As I came to the bell lap, Coach called out my split time of 8:40. I got a little confused with the math, thinking I had two laps left since I had never heard a seven lap split that low. I was concentrating too hard on running to do the math. I struggled a little bit from the fast pace through the turn and as I ran down the back straightaway, my teammates were hollering to kick it in. People in the backstretch bleachers were jumping up and down and screaming so I figured someone was coming up fast on my tail. I still had another gear to go, but I wanted to save it for what I thought was the next lap.

When I came in to the homestretch, everyone in the stands was clapping and yelling. Up ahead I could see the back end of the pack entering the turn and the meet officials brought out the finish tape to stretch across the line when the last of the runners went across the finish line.

Knowing now that I had miscounted the laps, I got up on my toes for a final sprint to the end. I could feel the crowd encouraging me on and was certain that a competitor was right on my heels. I broke the finish tape and ran on through the turn feeling like I could have easily gone another mile at the same speed if I had to.

I jogged to a stop and finally turned around to see who was behind. I was stunned to see the next group of runners just starting the finish straight, some hundred yards behind me. A meet official came up to me and showed me his stopwatch, which read 9:50.2.

I jogged on around the track to where a few of my

teammates were standing next to the fence separating the track from the bleachers and they held out their hands for me to slap high fives to as I ran by. I picked up my bag with my sweat suit and training flats and headed back to where my friends were standing.

I had never known a thrill quite like running as fast so effortlessly as I had just done. It was one of my first encounters with an almost magical state of being that comes with intense preparation, the exact right amount of recovery, the proper balance of endurance and speed training, and being primed mentally for a ferocious effort. Those days are few and far between for most athletes, but I had not learned this yet. I didn't really think too much about it at the time, because I just wanted to enjoy this feeling for as long as possible.

Which turned out to be not as long as I would have liked. The Regional meet was a few weeks later and this is where the top two finishers in each race qualify to compete in the State Championship meet. Our training had gone very well in the weeks leading up to it, but after my 2-mile at Boone County, I had a let-down in my mental toughness which I couldn't really put my finger on.

In a dual meet the following week, I ran a mile in 4:42 and then dropped out of the 880 with 220 yards to go. I did this for no apparent reason as I did not have any sort of injury or sickness. Coach Daley was not happy about it. It came as a shock to me too, because one minute I was struggling along feeling pretty bad and the next I was standing on the infield bending over to unlace my spikes. I was mad at myself and I could tell that several of my teammates were surprised to learn that I had any amount of quit in me.

Coach made me take a couple days of really easy training thinking that I was stale and needed a rest, but it was not enough to get me back to where I needed to be. At the Regional Meet, Coach decided to put me in the Mile and let Matt and Jude run the 2-mile with the anticipation that this gave us each the best chance to qualify for the State Meet. I ran a 4:35, but came in third, eliminating me from qualifying for State.

After my race, I did a couple of miles of running to cool down and arrived back at the area where my team was gathered. While I was out running on the road, I thought Coach would consider putting me in the 2-mile since I had the fastest time among my teammates, but I realized this wouldn't be fair to either of them since Coach had purposely held them out of the Mile with the hope that they would have fresh legs for their race.

It turned out that they both qualified to compete in the State Meet, and I was happy for them but I couldn't help but be mad at myself for not doing well enough in my race to join them. I finished out the next week practicing with the team and I competed one more time in the Conference Relays, running a 4:32 mile in the Distance Medley Relay which we won easily, breaking the Conference Distant Medley Record. The race was a statement for me in that I wanted to prove that I was still capable of racing well, but it was hard to tell whether I was trying to convince my Coach and teammates or myself.

I went as a spectator to the State Meet where my teammates who had qualified all ran well but didn't earn any medals. I was obviously unhappy not to be part of this competition, but my failures in the end of the track season would inspire me to go back to the drawing board as I prepared for the cross-country season ahead. My logbook pretty well sums it up in the "What I learned this season" notes I made on the last day of track season:

STEVE ADKISSON

1. *More mileage early in the season is helpful*
2. *No sox in races*
3. *I'm not a sophomore any more*
4. *No one is undefeatable*

III
JUNIOR

'It is all dying out in a voice asking,
"Where you from? How ya'll folks doing'?"
On the blank verse of the forklift man,
From way off down there and yonder,
Is draining, thou and thine, from prayers
Of spinsters in the Nazarene Church –
Is dying of knowledge of the world,
But still going, barely, in a grunted "hidey"
In the line at the cash register at Shoney's,
A father telling how he came north
To visit his son, impatience starting up
Its coughs behind him, his *yes 'ms* and *no 'ms*
An impediment here, Confederate money.
Kid's in my office, slow-talking. I ask,
"Where you from?" He doesn't seem to want
To say, thinks again, then does. "All over."'

From: "Elegy for the Southern Drawl"
-Rodney Jones

Being referred to as a redneck has not always contained the racial connotations it does today. As with many aspects of evolution in language, time has a way of altering meanings or connotations associated with words. Lloyd Memorial High School was one of the first schools in Kentucky to integrate and contained a large population of black students. After a decade of racial division in the 1960's, the 1970's became a time for raising awareness that there really was not much difference between human beings, regardless of the outer shell that covers them. Many older adults still used the words "negro" or "colored" when discussing the black race, but it always seemed to me to be just a descriptive word - like "short" or "long-haired" or "lanky," not as a way of degrading the person. It was just the descriptive words they learned in their upbringing.

My black friends preferred to be considered "black" rather than "African-American" and there was no expectation of reparation for the sins of white people hundreds of years ago. Their families had embraced their enfranchisement generations ago the same as mine had. The fact that there was such a thing as soul was obvious to anyone paying attention. We all had one – black or white. Some things go without saying.

The classrooms, ball fields, basketball courts, and hangouts where we met were places where there were seldom disagreements about anything other than whether a ball was fair or foul, if that elbow you took being boxed out was really a foul, or who was the meanest teacher in the school. We didn't ignore race, but we didn't really see a need to let it come between us.

No, "redneck" was a term used to describe people who spent a lot of time doing dirty jobs, who hunted and fished, worked on their own cars, farmed, knew how to operate heavy equipment, who were not intimidated by a nasty, hard job. I qualified in almost every category.

My family didn't have our own farm; in fact we lived

in what I learned later was a low income housing development. Both my parents were raised on farms and I had spent a lot of time around those farms since I was born. As a teenager, it was easy to get work from our friends and neighbors who farmed. I had learned to cut and hang tobacco, pitch hay, drive tractors, work with animals, and dig holes. My dad taught us gun safety and how to shoot about the same time we were learning to read. I cannot remember a time when a farmer I worked for didn't ask me to come back, which was the standard of how well you performed on the job.

My older brother and I were eight and six when my dad took a job in Cincinnati and moved our family of eight from Valley Station, Kentucky, a little town on the Ohio River west of Louisville. My youngest sister was born in the year after we moved to round out the family to seven kids. I had a pretty strong southern accent compared to the Yankee talk of other northern Kentucky kids and I became the target of their ridicule. In second grade, I told another kid at school I had a "hoe in mah pocket' and he made sure everybody knew to ask me where my lunch money went.

I had not lost much of the accent by the time I was in high school so I hid it pretty well by keeping my mouth shut most of the time, just to keep the hillbilly jokes to a minimum. My parents and most of my relatives are extremely intelligent people. It was annoying to have to defend my heritage based on the way I talked, so I chose just to avoid having to do it.

Coach Daley was from further south than I was, so he talked even slower and with more of an accent than I did. Maybe that was why I paid such close attention to him when he spoke, and defended him when my teammates tried to mock him. He did have some great southern sayings, which sounded funny in the context of running, but I understood them for the plainness of their language. When he told me "You can't go tearing out there like your head is on fire and your ass is trying to catch it!" I knew exactly what he meant. And when he told us we were "fixin to get whupped if you don't stop horsing around," everybody elevated their level of commitment.

He was definitely from the old school of coaching when it came to his absolute authority over the team, something his days of playing and coaching football had ingrained in his way of doing things. It was "my way or the highway" as far as Coach Daley was concerned. That was fine with me too because that was the same way the adult men in my family treated us and from the moment I began running, Coach Daley was there to guide and encourage me. He led a group of us from being a bunch of nervous knock-kneed colts, who may have had a competitive spirit and the willingness to work but lacked the structure and discipline to train smart, to championship starting lines and winners' circles. He devoted a great deal of his time and energy to learning more about the sport and teaching it to us. He was clever in his relationships with the media, and so was able to generate recognition for us without giving the other teams too much bulletin board material to rally against us.

But even more than that, Coach had a way of making us feel proud of doing the work it took to become a champion. It is one thing to be proud of accomplishing a goal that you set out to accomplish, to win meets and championships, but it is another thing completely to be proud of just doing the work it takes.

The inner redneck in me was just beginning to understand this.

In the summer of 1974, I went a little crazy. There is no real explanation for it. I turned 16 in the spring, fell in love with a girl, got my driver's license. I got in fights, mostly standing up for people being intimidated by a bully or harassed for their differences. My older brother was leaving for college so my status was upgraded to the oldest kid in the house. I stopped getting haircuts and shaving. I became a vegetarian. I read poems and enjoyed it, studied Zen and understood it. I was always a quiet person, but I became even more so. I had all the symptoms common to hippie drug addicts and from the looks and comments I was getting, I am pretty sure most people thought that's what I was becoming. Only the small handful of people who knew me well enough would have disputed that opinion.

People of all ages tend to blame their behavior and hardships on their parents. In a lot of cases, this is probably justified. My parents have always loved me and supported me in every endeavor I sought out. We had seven kids in my family and I don't think any one of them thinks they are not the favorite son or daughter. We weren't rich, but we were never hungry, neglected, or dirty. We were always expected to do our schoolwork to the best of our ability, to share the load of the chores in a large household, and to follow the fairly straightforward rules of behavior.

I guess I went crazy because there was an overwhelming amount of cultural change taking place in the 70's and I was just a hyper-energetic person who wanted to take in as much of the world as I possibly could. I read a lot and had friends who were older and wiser than me in the ways of the world and I made time to ask them questions and listen to their answers. I had already learned that much of what we are brainwashed to value in the world is sold to us on the television and through media advertising, which is ruthlessly manipulative. Once you become aware of this, you understand the simple premise that the world conspires to separate us from our money. I decided not to buy into it.

I started practicing yoga after reading some articles about it in Runner's World and watching my cousin Mark perform his yoga routine. I drove my mother nuts with being overly conscious about what I ate. She is an amazing cook and prepared literally every meal for nine people for the whole time I lived in the house. I am sure she did everything possible to accommodate me, but she was already preparing wholesome homecooked meals and there wasn't much she could have done differently.

When school started in August, I drove my teachers nuts by being contrary with their rules of behavior. I got my butt whacked by more teachers and administrators in the last two years of high school than any kid in my class. A lot of the times I got in trouble were because I would tell the truth about what had happened: "Yeah, we wrapped toilet paper all around Mr. So n So's car," or "Yes mam, I opened the window and let Jude in for homeroom so he wouldn't be counted tardy," or "Yes sir, I fell asleep. This class isn't all that interesting to me." Most students would try to weasel out of admitting responsibility for something they did, or blame it on someone else. I always figured it best just to come out with the straight truth, because it would be found out sooner or later. If given the choice between detention and three whacks on the butt, I always just turned around and bent over.

But I kept on running.

And as the summer of 1974 went by, I was more dedicated to becoming the best runner I could be than I had ever been before. I trained twice a day, every day. My brother John had decided to put his considerable athletic talents to work as a runner. He had fractured some vertebras in his back playing football as a freshman and the doctors told my mother he might be paralyzed if he had another injury to his back. She said no more football, so even though he was a starting linebacker and running back on the undefeated Freshman football team who would go on to win the State Football Championship his senior year, he started running with me almost every day. He had outgrown me in his first year of life and even though I was thirteen months older than him, people thought he was my older brother because he was considerably bigger than me.

Jude Baynum had an amazing track season and started the summer in excellent shape. He had found a new lucky red hat that he wore on every run. Jude and Gerry Baynum lived about a half mile from us and would run at any hour of the day or night with us. Gerry had started out as one of Coach Daley's junior high recruits and as his body matured, he had gotten faster and faster. He was 5' 8" and had the same easy stride as Jude. His curly dark hair had grown out to a passable afro and he always had a prank of some kind up his sleeve. We would run to their house and then continue on through town picking up others as we went out on our summer night runs. When the entire team was assembled, all of us would run four or five miles together. By the time John and I left our house, made our rounds to pick up everybody on our route, did a group run and then run home, we had easily covered eight or nine miles for our second run of the day.

Coach had emphasized that the State Championship held in early November was really won in July and August. I knew enough about training by then to believe this to be true so I made sure we had enough people on our team doing the training we needed to do to get ready for the 1974 cross-country season. I did not have to work very hard at it because we had at least ten guys who were really excited about running and we were having way too much fun doing it.

When I say I went crazy, I should temper it with the

fact that I was probably not the only one. It's hard to tell if insanity is contagious, but compared to several of my teammates I was maybe only in the top three.

Gerry Baynum, who was three years younger than his brother Jude and I, may not have actually been certifiably crazy but he sure was nuts. It may have been he had an inferiority complex from being the youngest in our group requiring him to constantly try to do something more outrageous than anything any of us older guys had ever done. One day before practice, Gerry came walking up in his peculiar "bigfoot with an attitude" stalking posture and he wasn't saying anything, which was unusual for him. He had this big stupid grin on his tight sealed lips. We watched as he approached and when he knew all eyes were on him, he pursed his lips and a snake poked its head out of his mouth. He let about three inches of a seven inch garter snake out and the snake waggled back and forth out of his mouth tasting the air with its tongue, while a dozen of us gagged, laughed, and howled.

Stuff like that.

Jude was a natural leader and was in unbelievable shape. He could run as far and fast as anybody wanted to go so when somebody on the team suggested we do a long run from our school down to Big Bone Lick State Park, he was all for it. The plan was to run to the park and meet up with Jeff's mom who would bring our camping gear, food, and water. We would camp at the park and she would come back the next morning to pick us up and ride us home.

Nobody really knew how far it was before we set off on the run, so we were a little surprised to learn that Jeff's mom measured it at 17 miles. We left school at 7:00 a.m. and two hours later, four of us were sprinting ahead of the other half dozen runners who had been crazy enough to set out on this long run.

JUGGERNAUTS

The next morning, I got up early and went out for a 9 mile run around the park's trail system. When I got back, John said he was going to run home. Jeff's mom arrived to drive us home and I decided to go ahead and take the van back home, but when Jeff saw that John was serious about running back to Erlanger, he refused to be outdone and put his camping gear in the van and the two of them ran home.

The very next day, the rest of us did the same 17 mile run again – just on principle.

It wasn't long after these Big Bone Runs in July when the concept that every day's run had to be an adventure started to manifest itself. One of the phenomena about being in extremely good physical shape is that it takes longer and longer runs to wear you out. In our case, knowing that 17 miles was easily within our capabilities, there was virtually an unlimited amount of trouble we could get into in the span of two hours of running the streets and trails around our town. The city only spans about three miles by five miles so in a single run, we could easily cover the distance between any two points. Since many of us worked full time in the summer, it was not unusual to begin a run at 11:30 p.m. when the second shift ended.

And like I said, every run became an adventure.

When school started my junior year, I discovered I had developed an interest in acquiring knowledge, but not necessarily the kind they taught at school. Over the summer I read Ayn Rand's Atlas Shrugged and Herman Hesse's book Siddhartha and recognized for the first time that I was, in fact, on a quest to discover my path – whether that was what I was calling it or not. Among other things, the awareness that there is such a thing as "a path," and that it was my destiny to walk it, made me treat each interaction I had with another human being as an opportunity to learn what that person had to teach me. The learning has proven to be endless.

I took a college bound curriculum so I was required to take Biology, Chemistry, Algebra, as well as the standard English and History classes every high school requires. I had several teachers who took a particular interest in nurturing this newly acquired thirst for knowledge. That or my reputation for poor "deportment" had preceded me and they were just making a good attempt at keeping me occupied. Mr. Hinsdale, who was also the new assistant cross-country coach, emphasized writing in his English class and required me to put words together in an order that would allow others to know what I was thinking inside my head. He forbade any form of plagiarism and could tell easily if someone's homework assignment had been improved with outside assistance.

He also loaned out his personal books, including those of Joseph Conrad, Faulkner, and several poets who were still alive and writing, some of them even in Kentucky! I had been led to believe that all the real poets had died a long time ago, based on the teachings of the English texts used in all my schooling up until then.

When one of my class mates admitted he needed some work on his "vocabularity", the concept of the "Word of the Day" became a reality for everybody in the class. Each day a new word was written on the board and we were required to write that word in a notebook and look up its meaning. The words were selected for their obscurity in common use. At the end of the week, a quiz would be given with the definitions as the "question" and you had to give the correct word as the answer. All of the words were in the English language, but you could have fooled me about half the time. Words like: *recapitulate, moiety, orthography, jejune, and laissez faire.* The effect of this on me and my teammates in the class was that we turned these words loose on the rest of the team. We tried, often without success, to use one of these big words when a smaller one would have done the job just as well. These "words of the day" found their way into my log book when they were particularly funny or when they had been misused in our discussions in a remarkable way, or if someone's circumlocution was particularly outrageous.

> *Sept 15 – a.m. 5 miles O.L. at an easy pace. Jude wondered if Gerry's eating 10 pieces of pizza right before heading out for a run would have a "deleterious" affect on his performance. Steve N said it may just "gerrymander" his innards.*
> *Oct 23– a.m. 2 miles easy (tired) p.m. 6 miles hard on trails. Gerry said "Jude was home being lugubrious because he was sick." Nite: 2 miles We stopped by to give him some grief.*

Another teacher, Ms. Ellis, had an English class for upper classman called "Free Reading" and she would recommend books to those of us who were interested. Other students in the class would recommend books they liked and there were several of the smartest kids in the school in the class. Among those was my friend Alice, the writer. She introduced me to the Tolkien trilogy, Helen Keller, as well as poets like Robert Frost, T.S. Elliot, and W.S. Merwin. All the class required was that you appeared to be reading and then you were required to write a book report on the book you had read. This gave me a chance to both read and write for the required school credit, something I would have probably found time to do on my own since I enjoyed doing it anyway.

The other influence on our learning was the television series *Kung Fu*, which the team would gather to watch at our house every Thursday night. We would sit quietly and wait for either Master Po or Master Kahn to make their enlightened statements about the challenges a monk faces. I would translate this inside my head from its application to a monk in ancient China to my day-to-day challenges as a Kentucky kid pursuing excellence as a runner. I started to think of my daily training as austerities that were building strength and energy which could be called upon later. I probably took this more seriously than many of my teammates who mostly looked forward to the part of the show when Kwi Chang Cain would invariably put on his orange pajamas and beat the crap out of some unenlightened lawman, bad guy, or Shaolin assassin come to take him out.

My thirst for knowledge also led me to take my studies seriously enough that I wanted to make A's. I developed a habit of simply paying close attention in class, reading the assignment or doing the practice problems once, and then concentrating hard at test time. I was never much on studying or trying to kiss up to a teacher in class to get on their "good side." I figured I either knew the stuff or I didn't and my grade would tell in the end.

One biology teacher, Mr. Blankenbaker, brought a certain eccentricity to his teaching. One of his many quirks was to tap a big beaker filled halfway up with water with a ruler as his signal to move to another station during his lab quizzes. It made a sound like a brass bell, a sound which gave him great joy judging by the broad smile it brought to his face each time he hit the glass. He was big on making sure we understood the Scientific Method of determining if a certain theory was true. He went to great lengths to have us work through the process of taking a theory and proving whether it was true or not. He was less concerned with having us memorize the nomenclature of biology than that we had a grasp on the larger principles of science. We were given assignments that required us to hypothesize and perform an experiment testing the hypothesis. Some of the basic human anatomy and physiologic principles were particularly interesting to me as I continued to learn more about being a runner.

But even before I had taken his class explaining the scientific method and the various ways to test a theorem, we had been experimenting with the way the body reacts to a variety of stresses and external conditions.

There are few rewards of a long run in the summer's heat that rival a quick dip into a pool. There is even an Endothermic Principle in Physics that describes the release of heat from one body of mass to another called the "Whoo Theorem" or possibly the "Wu Theorem", I really don't remember. We usually just said "WooHoo!" The easiest way to understand the principle is to perform the following experiment which we performed on many occasions during or after our summer runs.

The experiment starts with the basic premise that you must first warm a body of mass to a suitable temperature above its normal state. In the case of the bodies involved in this experiment, that core temperature starts out at 98.6. When you run ten or twelve miles on a July evening in Kentucky, that temperature can be increased considerably. The attained temperature is rarely known in precise terms, but for the sake of discussion we will use the terms described in Table 1 below:

Table 1

Temperature	Terminology
98.6F	Cold Blooded
99.6	Warming Up
100.6	About Good
101.6	Worked Up A Pretty Good Sweat
102.6	Geeze, Man It's Hot!
103.6	Let's Stop & Get A Drink
104.6	How Far Is It To The Pool

Once the subject's core body temperature reaches a core temperature of 104.6 F, his only conscious thought thereafter is "How Far Is It To The Pool." This usually means he has about 5 minutes of consciousness left before he must submerge himself into a liquid mass of specific temperature, hopefully considerably below his own, or risk heat stroke.

Now, having sufficiently warmed the subjects to somewhere between "Worked Up A Pretty Good Sweat" and "How Far Is It To The Pool," we invented a game in which the participants must find the nearest pool and dive in, the objective being to get the body temperature to "About Good" without having the police called. If you are a group of poor kids in the suburban neighborhoods of northern Kentucky, you intentionally set out for the parts of town where there are pools, and conveniently, where nobody knows you. The run to these suburbs on your average July night is performed in 85 degree temperatures with 90% humidity and you are doing good to go three miles before your body reaches "Geeze, Man It's Hot" temperature.

One summer night in 1974, a record sixteen pools were accomplished in a single run. Of course, some of the pools were in the back yards of houses where the occupants were on vacation, but other homes were fully occupied with the owners taken by complete surprise at the multiple loud splashes coming from their back yards.

The real trick to making it into the Pool Hopping Hall of Fame is to pick a group of runners motivated more by stealth than by adrenaline. Of course, this became harder and harder to do on our team. On this particular night all the right conditions came together for what would have had to be described as a "Perfect Game" in baseball.

I had just returned home from my 3:00 p.m. to 11:00 p.m. job as a bellman at the Holiday Inn, and my brother John was sitting in the light of the porch lacing up his shoes when I pulled into the driveway. He announced that the Baynum brothers were waiting for us so I quickly changed into shorts and shoes and we were on our way.

The Baynums lived about a half mile away and even though the lighting was never good on that stretch of road, we ran in the dark and were there in just a few minutes. Already we were approaching the "About Good" zone when Gerry announced we were going for the record.

"What is the record?" I asked him, thinking we were going to attempt a course record time for one of our regular runs.

"Eight," he said, with that stupid grin on his face.

"Eight what?" I asked.

"Eight pools." The same stupid grin.

"Who did eight?" I had to know.

"Me." Same stupid grin.

We ran on silently in contemplation of this fact. Jude, Johnny, and I knew that Gerry never bragged or exaggerated, especially about his own personal accomplishments. For him to state that he had hopped into eight different pools in one night meant that he had doubled our known group effort of four which was done more as a small prank (and all in apartment pools where there is little danger of consequence other than being told to leave). The week before we did a night run which took us by several apartment complexes. We simply walked in like we lived there, took off our shoes and jumped in, got out, dried off, put on our shoes and went on down the road. In repeating this a few more times, we had a memorable and pleasant evening of running and been kept reasonably comfortable in the heat by our short submersions.

The number eight rumbled around in that same unfathomable stratosphere as Roger Maris's 61 home runs, Ty Cobb's 4192 base hits, John Walker's 3:49 mile, or Wilt Chamberlain's 100 points in a basketball game. All three of us ran on beside Gerry in awe and amazement.

All three of us were thinking, and two of us said, the same thing at the same time:

ÒThat ain't nothin.Ó

"We could do 16, easy!" said Jude, who was Gerry's older brother after all and never to be outdone.

"There ain't that many pools in town," Johnny, ever the thinking man, said.

"How deep does a pool have to be to count?" I asked after an uncomfortable pause in which we were calculating the many variables in our heads.

No one answered immediately. It was our game and we made up the rules. This was not something to be taken lightly. The future of organized sports and any later attempt to break a record stood poised on the wisdom of this one crucial decision.

It is commonly known that great minds think alike, as we had demonstrated just a half-mile back in analyzing Gerry's record. This principle was at work again when we all came up with the answer: "We could count lakes," we said, almost in unison.

JUGGERNAUTS

No cartographer of the area could have drawn a clearer picture of our route than the one that was forming itself in my mind. I quickly did an out of body travel thing placing myself about three miles above the surface of the earth and I could see the many lakes that I had sneaked into to fish, or ice skated on in the winter, or had raced around in the various meets held within a five mile radius of where we were now running. There were no less than eight I could think of: three on the golf course, two in the cemetery, two on farms, and several others in the neighborhood we were approaching.

We stopped for a moment waiting for the sparse traffic to clear on the four lane Dixie Highway, the major north-south road which runs from Canada to Florida and passes right through Erlanger. Though there are stop lights every quarter mile or so to manage the heavy commuter traffic, at this time of night there was seldom any cars on it.

Our wills were being solidified about what our next step should be. We had run five miles that morning at 6:00. All four of us had worked our regular full time jobs sometime that day and knew we had to get up again the next day to go back to work. It was eleven thirty on a week night, hot and not showing any signs of cooling off. A lesser group might have considered turning back and trying on another night when conditions would be more conducive to the effort it might take to accomplish what lay ahead.

No one had the courage nor wisdom to filibuster our already stated plan, so when the traffic cleared, Gerry sprinted across and hollered behind him: "You all going swimming with me or not!"

The line in the sand had been crossed. The race was on. Within a few minutes we were sprinting across the field toward the banks of Silver Lake, which was bordered by land owned by a pretty nice family who welcomed the community to fish or skate but probably wouldn't have cared much for the midnight skinny-dipping about to occur there. At this first lake, we took off our shoes and what were still relatively dry shorts, before slipping into the water and getting fully submerged. The only rule that was crystal clear for all of us was that no body of water that you couldn't go completely into would count as a "pool."

Having our first pool easily completed we hurriedly dressed and put on our shoes and within a half mile came to a house Jude said had a pool in the backyard. With the stealth of Navy seals, we slipped through the dark side yard and stopped to peek around the back corner of the house. Sure enough there was a pool. Gerry leaned over to start untying his shoes, but Johnny reached down and touched his shoulder. Gerry looked up and Johnny shook his head no and pointed to his wristwatch. All three of us got the message and another codification of official pool hopping was established. "Shoes are permitted to be worn when conditions exist where a hasty exit may be necessary," is how this section would have read had the rules ever been written down.

All four of us leaned and began an army crawl toward the inground pool and within a few seconds all four of us had another pool and were crawling across the yard when the back porch light came on and a man came out carrying a baseball bat.

"What the . . .?" was the last thing I heard as we jumped up and bolted toward the street. My heartrate bounced up to about 220 plus my age and continued on into the redline area as we sprinted down the street to an unlit section of road and assumed no one was following us. Having escaped without consequence made us at first giddy, then breathless, then as we slowed down to a pace where we could talk again, the whole incident became uproariously funny.

JUGGERNAUTS

Once the laughter subdued, I asked Jude how he knew there was a pool there when none of the rest of us knew anyone who lived in that part of town, he answered in the best suave voice he could muster: "One of my girlfriends lives there."

"How many girlfriends do you have?" John asked him, knowing that Jude had a steady girlfriend at school.

"A pair and a spare," Jude answered, as if that should have been a well known bona fide fact.

Johnny thought this answer over for a minute and said: "Hang on. We have to go back."

"I ain't going back," I said, ever the smarter, older brother.

"Not to that house," he said. "I know a girl who lives a few houses down from where we just were, and *she* has a pool."

"Nuh unh?" Gerry said.

"No foolin," Johnny said.

And sure enough, a few minutes later, he raised a finger to his lips and pointed between two yards on the opposite side of the street from where we had just recorded our second pool. There behind the house was what we would learn over the next year to be the pool hopper's nightmare: an above ground pool. The reasons for this would seem obvious once they are thought through, but the thinking through of things was not something we were all that good at.

The first potential for problems is that elevated pools typically have a deck or platform built around them with an entrance to that deck coming right out the back door of the house. Building codes typically require a 36 inch tall guardrail around the pool area to keep non-swimming youngsters safely away. This layout provides a particular challenge in that entrance is strictly limited to going right by the door of the house and egress is accomplished either the same way or

103

by jumping off the deck or fencing around the elevated pool.

People who have permission to use the pool never think about these things, but people who don't have permission must learn to roll when they hit the ground after jumping from six or seven feet above it. Which is pretty much what we had to do after Johnny, Gerry, and myself slipped quietly into the pool, only to discover that Jude had climbed up on top of the tool shed next to the pool and given his horrifying "Laugh of Death" as he cannonballed into it.

Before the owner of the pool had a chance to wipe the sleep out his eyes and grab his weapon of choice, we were out of his pool anyway and 200 yards down the street, dripping, laughing, and taking turns punching at Jude who had caught and passed us. He was obviously proud in his accomplishment.

Sensing that our morale was getting a little too good, I suggested that we better be careful. No one acknowledged hearing a word I said.

I myself was beginning to get a feeling something magical was taking place, that the moon and alignment of the planets was such that there might be no stopping us tonight, that maybe, just maybe, those . . . . blue lights up ahead weren't mounted on top of a police car!

"Shoot!" said Johnny.

"Dang!" said Jude.

"We're busted," said Gerry.

"This way!" I said.

Knowing the only way this cop could catch us was if he was in his car, and that cars mostly only go on roads, I ducked in between the two nearest houses and proceeded at a dead sprint through the yards and into the woods behind the house. It was dark under the canopy of trees, but there was enough light to navigate through the trees just out of sight of our pursuer.

For many years I have pondered the question: Can you run faster if you're scared or if you're mad? After a seemingly endless volume of personal experience, I can assure you it is fear that lights the jets like nothing else. Olympic sprinters can have all the steroids, HGH, and other performance enhancing substances they want if they'll just give me a little of my own natural adrenaline, the kind that comes on suddenly and you don't notice it until you start paying attention to the fact that you seem to be sailing six feet off the ground and you look back for your buddies and they are fifty yards behind you starting to believe you've ditched them and getting pretty pissed about it.

In what seemed like a half-hour but was probably a minute we emerged from the woods into the back yard of a home that had, and I know you probably won't believe this: an above ground pool! Catching our breath in the shadow of the trees and listening for signs of any followers or potential problems with #4, we huddled together and sat looking back over our shoulders, or at the pool, or at the house. After a minute or so, we silently determined that it was OK to go on and we slipped into the pool by going over the side, dunked under, and slipped out in such a quiet and stealthy manner that we never even saw the man sleeping on his outdoor recliner next to his pool until we squished along side the pool and Johnny poked Jude and pointed at him.

For an instant I thought they would not be able to resist dumping him into the pool but they somehow found the will to resist and we proceeded on our quest.

Having tied the previous group record of four pools (we were calling the lakes pools by virtue of the unanimous decision of the board of regulators, i.e. us), we proceeded on to the golf course where no fewer than three lakes were easy prey at this time of night.

Forty minutes, eleven shortcuts, and seven pools later, we made our way to the apartment complexes whose pools were more or less lined up a quarter-mile apart and access entailed the simple hop of a low fence. We were getting pretty good at diving in, swimming the width of the pool and pulling ourselves out without breaking stride and the fourteenth pool had been accomplished in a total time of a little over an hour and twenty minutes. We had been in serious danger of apprehension only once. Our skin was starting to prune up and most of us had various scrapes, slightly twisted ankles, or cuts from the fences, but all in all, we were nearly overwhelmed with pride.

We had stopped thinking about where the next pool was, as each of us now knew the subliminal route that had formed in our collective subconscious. The last two bodies of water were on our way home and one of them belonged to a friend's family who would not be shocked too much if we were found in their pool at 1:00 in the morning.

The second to last was to be in the shade cooled waters of Garbett's Lake,which was nestled in the woods behind Garbett's Greenhouse, a mere half mile from our house. The other three didn't know it, but I had my one and only blast of rocksalt from a shotgun fired in my direction by Mr. Garbett, who was none too pleased to catch me fishing in his lake at sunrise one morning a few years back. I left a pretty decent stringer of bluegills behind, too.

But as we grew nearer to the lake, a real reluctance came over me to venture into the woods and sneak down next to the lake. Call it a sixth sense, or being overly cautious, but something, one of those voices, was telling me that this was not a good place for me to be. As you might imagine, there was no sharing of my concern with the present company. It was too dark to see their eyes, but I could sense the steely-eyed resolve that existed because when we said sixteen, we meant sixteen. Fifteen would not do.

So I did what any sixteen-year-old under this kind of pressure would do: I followed my peers into the woods, squished down to the lake, and walked into the water. I floated on my back out into the deeper part of the lake and looked up at the stars. I remember the low gurgling sound you can hear with your ears under water of others swimming nearby and I remember how loud the crickets sounded when I leaned forward and lifted my head out of the water. I turned to see the white teeth in the beaming smiles of my brother and friends and now I could only hear that one voice inside that was saying "Yes, yes you can," when the thirty-seven other voices that talk to us constantly were all saying their variations of "No, you can't."

And a half-mile later, after our last chlorine bath in the pool belonging to neighbors who welcomed pretty much any of their kids' friends anytime, I stood under a street light with my brother and my friends.

"Pretty decent run," Gerry understated, with that fatuous grin.

"Sixteen!" Johnny said.

"I'm starving," Jude added.

The Baynums turned toward their house and slogged off to make another in a long series of attacks on their mom's refrigerator. Johnny and I started the quarter mile walk up the hill to our house. It was dark; the only sound was the crickets, the hum of the streetlights, and the squishing of water in our every step.

Jeff Odgen and John Adkisson snacking on grasshopper.
Spectator Yearbook photo.

JUGGERNAUTS

"Once the last trace of emotion has been eradicated, nothing remains of thought but absolute tautology."

-Theodore W. Adorno,
German composer and sociologist

After a great summer of training, mostly twice a day
sessions of 3-6 miles in the morning and 5-10 miles in the
afternoon, we finally started formal team practices on the
first day of August. Coach Daley had sent home a training
schedule on the last day of school for us to follow through
the summer and most of us followed that schedule to the
letter or had in fact done even more mileage. On the first
day of practice, Coach had us meet at 7:00 p.m. at the big
maple tree in front of school where we usually met for
practice.

John, Jude, Gerry, and I ran up to school that day just
because we were used to getting out and running. Most of
the other runners had arrived when we ran up and they
were all watching as we jogged by the amphitheater and up
the hill to the maple tree.

"Well I see some of you can't hardly get enough,"
Coach joked as we joined the group of twenty-five athletes
sitting on the lawn waiting for practice to begin.

Coach had a box full of papers and his clipboard lying
on the ground beside him. He looked over the bunch of
runners and then over at me as if to say "Can you believe
this?"

Coach worked as a Physical Education teacher in the
middle school and had done a great job of recruiting. He
administered the President's Physical Fitness Test every
year, which consisted of having the PE students perform
their maximum number of pull-ups, sit-ups, and run the 50

and 600 yard dashes. When a student showed promise of success or talent at running, he invited him to come out for cross-country the following year. Sitting there before him were at least a dozen such students who had forsaken the glory of a promising football career, and signed on to become runners.

He knew I had been there that first year with him and had seen the phenomenal growth of interest in running. He was very proud of building this interest but he was also too modest to take much credit for accomplishing it.

"Now fellas, I want to go over the rules for being on the cross-country team", he began. I'd heard this speech twice already so I was interested to see how he set the newcomers straight. Coach and I had a pretty simple understanding. I knew he was the absolute ruler and he knew I was going to give him everything I had. I chuckled inside as he went through his ritual of stating the rules.

"Be on time. Last year somebody decided they were gonna give a note to a girl after school and they ended up getting left behind when the bus left school for Devou Park. I don't have time to waste waiting around for you to get to practice. If you get detention and can't come to practice, tell somebody on the team. Chances are, I'm gonna want to talk to the teacher who gave you detention. If you're messing up that bad in school, I may not want you on the team."

The younger runners were looking around at each other.

"The other thing is: I will treat you like a man if you treat me like a man. By that I mean, I understand that there are things that go on in life that are more important than running. If you have a problem, come to me and tell me about it. I can't read minds.

"We have an outstanding team this year. Some of you new people are going to have a hard time keeping up with the older guys. I understand that. The way to improve is to stick around for a couple of years and work your butt off like some of the older fellas have done. Our goal is to win the State Championship and that means we hope to send our best seven runners to the State Meet in Louisville at the end of the year. I don't play any games with who we send. The seven runners who have the fastest times in the Regional Meet will go to State."

"I want this to be clear right from the get-go so nobody's feelings get hurt. We are going to have ten or twelve of you competing for those top seven spots. When we run meets, the Junior Varsity runs the same course as the Varsity so if the first few JV runners have better times than the last couple of Varsity runners, they will move up to Varsity at the next meet.

"Is that clear to everybody?"

Coach stepped back and let his comments sink in. I knew he had thought this speech through because it was the longest one he had ever given to us. He was foreseeing the way the sheer number of talented athletes was going to push everyone to improve over the next couple of months and how the competition was going to be very intense.

He waited to see if anyone asked questions, but after a few minutes of head nodding, he said, "Ok then. Let's get going."

Logbook Aug 1974

August 1 1 mile warmup 4 miles in 24:32 5x150 fast
August 2 Went to Kings Island – walked 15 miles!
August 3 2 miles very easy
August 4 Jr. Olympic 1 Mile – 1ˢᵗ 4:38 slow first 880
August 7 Aft. 5 miles fartlek in rain felt great Evening
*   10 miles around golf course. .*

111

August 16 Butler Park 10 miles with 5 x 440 fast en-
route . . .
August 17 Butler Park a.m. 8 ½ miles road race 44:27
p.m. 6 miles fartlek . . .
August 20 8 miles hard fartlek at Summit Hills golf
course
Eve 2 mile time trial 10:15

The Baynum Brothers, Gerry & Jude.
After a home meet 1974.
Spectator Yearbook photo.

Nine times out of ten the difference between winning and losing doesn't come down to talent. It always comes down to who wanted it the most to begin with. Not just at the moment a race is being decided, or when the final seconds tick off – but months, sometimes years, earlier. This is especially true of distance running. The race is just a continuation of the months or years of wanting to be a winner.

None of the best runners on our team had talent, or some extra chromosome, in the sense that you could just look at them and tell they were anything but ordinary. Matt was average height and had a strong upper body from years of competitive swimming. Steve was also a swimmer, tall and built on a large frame. Jeff, J.C., and Dave were tall and lean but ungraceful in their running gaits. John was built like a linebacker and Gerry was average height and weight, but had a power running style that didn't look like he could last very long. Herald was graceful and smooth, but skinnier than any of us. Denny was strong and powerful, but he had a bulldozer style of muscling along. Jude and I were little and wiry, built more like beagles than greyhounds.

It is said that being a champion is just a decision you make – but you have to make the decision every single day. You have to wake up thinking about what you can do today to make yourself better. And then you have to spend all day doing those things, which more often than not requires hard work and trading the hours that most people spend on leisure activities for hours of disciplining yourself in running, stretching, or resting. You have to be comfortable leaving the comfort zone. Lots of people can endure the hard work. And just as many are willing to put in the long hours of training, do the strength and flexibility exercises, stick to a wholesome and mostly unexciting diet, and sacrifice a normal social life all in the interest of running further and faster. But that is still not enough to separate the winners from the rest of the pack.

The true determining factor is a rare ability to push the body through pain that evolution has designed into the body as a survival mechanism. When muscles perform, they begin at a state of balance in a complex system of fuels, gases, and liquids of which the human body is composed. At this point, you feel good.

The body in motion operates much like a furnace. Muscles burn fuels and as with any fire, they need oxygen for this process. In respiration, we take in oxygen when we inhale and we put out exhaust in the form of carbon dioxide

113

as we exhale. The fuel, the oxygen, and exhaust are all carried around in our bodies through the blood.

After several minutes of warming up, the body is humming along at its most efficient. The fuel it needs for muscles to fire is being processed with the available amount of oxidized blood, and the blood is able to carry the exhaust away at the same rate it is being generated. A trained athlete feels better after he has reached this phase.

You go a little further and a little faster and the body gauges are reaching the cruise mode. It is taking in just enough oxygen, has enough fuel, and is able to carry away the byproducts fast enough, but just barely. Discomfort begins to enervate all the systems. An unfit person usually stops here. A trained athlete can push further but would like to slow down to let the exhaust clear out. Muscles begin to feel weaker because lactic acid is accumulating in the blood stream. Your legs feel heavy. Your lungs are struggling to expel the built up carbon monoxide while your chest heaves in and out in an attempt to take in more oxygen from the hemoglobin in the bloodstream. This is the body's survival mechanism sending the signals to the muscles that continued exertion would endanger the organism. The brain is also an oxygen eater and it sends all the signals to the other parts of the body that if they continue using all the oxygen, the brain will have to quit. In other words, the brain tells everything else to shut down and you pass out so the blood can work its miracle of reestablishing the state of balance that it is continuously trying to maintain.

This is the point a champion is able to push through. He is able to get right up to the point where the brain is screaming "No more" and then go just a little bit further. But then, there is another difference. Some are able to recover quickly by virtue of having pushed the body to its breaking point and recovering from it enough times that

114

they know they will survive. This is a hard gained state of being that is only arrived at by repeatedly pushing the body hard enough to reach that place where your lungs are burning, the legs feel like they weigh a hundred pounds apiece, and your arms and shoulders are tingling.

The real champions are able to do this and like it. They may not admit to anyone that they enjoy this, but they are homogeneous in that they secretly derive a perverse pleasure in taking their body repeatedly to its breaking point. Denny said one time that he thought our 20 x 440 workout was like hitting himself in the head with a hammer – "It feels good when you stop."

For distance runners, the daily discipline required adds even another dimension to the enjoyment factor. Because year around training by definition takes place in all seasons, there are very few actual ideal days from a weather standpoint. You often find yourself in the rain, in strong winds, in very hot or very cold conditions. The unpleasantness of just being out in some of these less-than-ideal environments, let alone pushing yourself to exhaustion, is enough to build character in those that survive.

It was rare to hear a complaint from any one on our team about the weather or the amount of mileage or intensity of training runs. If anyone even hinted at the thought that it was too hot, or too cold, or too whatever outside to go for a run, they would immediately be shot down with the team's motto: "Don't be a wussy." Only we didn't say wussy.

STEVE ADKISSON

"How old would you be
if you didn't know how old you was?"

-Satchel Paige,
Negro League Hall of Fame Pitcher

I am not sure what it is about the name a parent gives a child that makes it necessary to expurgate that name when the child becomes a teenager. It seems that every kid I grew up with found himself being called something else by the time they turned fifteen. Of course, I grew up mostly being a runner, so most of my friends had their given names bowdlerized by someone else on the team.

I was both the victim and perpetrator of this process. Earning a nickname is one of those things that normally just happens spontaneously, and the best nicknames are the ones that are exactly right for either the person who is fitted with it or the event that is immortalized in the never-to-be-forgotten nickname. This is especially true if the recipient doesn't particularly like the nickname he is given.

Gerry, for example, got his nickname Beaves, because he was the younger brother of Jude Baynum, and every annoying little brother was easily tagged with the Beaver Cleaver name from the show *Leave It To Beaver* After a while, even Beave's own mother got to where she called him that too.

That I ever knew of, he never claimed to dislike it, but it probably became an obstacle to getting dates when he grew out of that cute little brother phase of his life.

We called Gary Graves "Gravedigger" which was a no brainer. Steve Nienaber was "Knee." We called Denny Heidrich "Hendrix". Doug Vagedes was "Bag Of Fleas." These were all the easy ones.

JUGGERNAUTS

There is probably a "Wedgie" in every crowd of kids. We called whoever was the biggest pain in the butt "Wedgie" and if you were a younger kid hanging out with the older guys, you had to be on guard to avoid doing anything to earn you that name. That was one you wouldn't really want to stick.

One of the surest ways to get a nickname that would stick was to do something Coach would end up hollering at you about. He had a way of just mentioning something in passing that someone would overhear and our photographic memories would bring it up later and the name might as well have been tattooed on the forehead of the person.

A nickname of this variety was earned on one of our weekend cross-country camps. Coach had made the mistake of going to sleep about 11:00 p.m. in the privacy of the officers' quarters at the Army National Guard camp, and left us upperclassmen in charge of getting everybody settled down. Coach knew we had all run about 15 miles that day, including several long hill repeats. We had swum for several hours in the lake, and being the second night of camp, he figured we had to be wearing out.

And he was mostly correct, except that he underestimated our ability to function without adequate sleep. In one of our crueler treatments of an underclassman, Jude, Beaves, and I had tricked an eighth grader into going outside the building and shut the door on him. Now, if you have never been out in the muggy heat of an August night in the Kentucky River Valley, you would have no idea of the misery that quickly engulfed young Darren Suter. Suter had been pretty much of a Wedgie to us for the entire trip, and he did have it coming to him, but we probably overpunished him for the offenses he had committed. Kentucky mosquitoes are famous for their ability to inflict excruciating welts. To be bitten a half dozen times while sitting on

117

the porch is usually warning enough to retreat to the safety of a shelter. We shut Darren out into the swarm with just his underwear and the blanket he had wrapped around him.

We locked the door on him and had planned to go back to the door and check on him later, but as coach had assumed – we were tired. And we did fall asleep.

When we woke up the next morning, we had completely forgotten about young Suter. Coach sent us off on a 9-mile run, and somewhere in the middle of that run when our brains were starting to wake up, somebody asked where Darren was. I ran on in contemplation of this question. In reconstructing the morning, I remember that we had all left the building through the same door that we had locked him out of, but distinctly remember not seeing him anywhere around the grounds. I started worrying maybe he had walked the two miles to town, called his mom, and would be waiting with her when we arrived back at the camp. Even then, what we had done could have been construed as bullying a weaker, younger student and we would have been harshly disciplined.

I didn't say anything. Jude edged up beside me as we ran and asked what I thought had happened to Darren, but I just shrugged my shoulders. I was seriously starting to worry about what had become of him.

We finished the run, showered, and went in to town to eat breakfast at Coach's favorite greasy spoon. Coach didn't really have much of a budget for our cross-country team, so it was every one for himself. Most of us had brought money to eat on, and if anybody was short, somebody with a little extra would loan them a couple bucks. There were probably twenty of us at this camp, so coach didn't really miss one kid. Some of us were old enough to drive and coach was confident that everyone who wanted to come out to eat would have been resourceful enough to manage a ride in to town.

After breakfast, we returned to the Army National Guard Base and coach had us tidy up the place a little. I had been raised to make my bed upon leaving it, so all my gear was already in order. Several of us just went outside to hang out while we waited on the others. Coach came out and was standing under the big shade tree talking with us when I saw him look out on the horizon toward the river-bank. He squinted his eyes and held his gaze in that direction, which caused all of us to turn our heads to look at whatever it was he was seeing.

Out of the woods about a half mile away came walking a 13 year old kid in his underwear dragging a gray felt blanket across the grass. I knew right away who it was, but was surprised by the direction he was coming from. As he got close enough to see him, I could see his whole upper body was one big welt. His eyes were swollen halfway shut and his forehead had knots the size of marbles on it.

Coach was starting to put together a possible explana-tion, but as soon as Darren got close enough to hear him, coach says, "Where in the hell have you been?"

Suter turned around and pointed. "I fell asleep in the woods."

Coach looked him over and shook his head. "I don't know what we're going to do with you son. You keep play-ing like Rip Van Winkle and you're gonna find yourself left down here when we leave." Coach turned and walked back in to check on the progress of the clean up.

I kind of felt bad for Rip Van Winkle. He looked awful. I can only imagine the miserable night he must have had. I guess he figured the farther away from the lights he could get, the fewer bites he would have to endure. Of course he didn't realize this for several hours after he had been shut out. He must have wriggled around in agony until his body grew so tired that nothing could keep him awake before he finally dozed off. Being that tired, and with the mosquitoes finally gone when the sun came up, he had slept until nearly noon.

I don't believe he ever held the events of that night against us. We eventually shortened his nickname to a simple "Winkle." He actually worshipped Beaves who was closer to his age and the two of them were good friends for their remaining years running together. But he steered clear of Jude and me for quite a while afterwards, even though we made it clear to him that we respected him for not "naming names" when he had a pretty good reason to make us pay.

The nickname eventually given to me deserves an explanation. Even though I brought a nickname with me from elementary school, the one my teammates gave me has managed to stick. A seventh grade history teacher had called me "Speedy" when I had promptly delivered his attendance slip to the office and returned in what must have seemed to him a comparatively short time. I had simply walked the paper to the office, handed it to the secretary, and walked straight back to the room. He must have been comparing my walking pace to the stop-at-the-water-fountain, look-around-the-office, stop-at-the-restroom type of delivery service that was common among my peers. I had yet to even run a track or cross-country race.

Anyway, some of my fellow students heard him call me this, and it hung on for a while. But my real friends called me by my given name until the day I earned the nickname they thought I was really worthy of.

A series of events led up to the name. Over the course of several years I had become known for participating in elaborate pranks that required planning beyond simply grabbing an armful of rotten tomatoes from the garden and heading out for a night of 'matering, or setting a paper bag full of dog fecal matter on fire and ringing a doorbell. Sure, these were common pranks of the day, and I must admit that I have been present at the execution of some of these. But the really good ones that required some pre-scouting and precision planning had become second nature to me by the time I had been running for three years.

Even though I didn't actually drive the big rubber tired articulating front-end loader onto the school amphitheater one night (it had been my younger brother) a lot of people figured it was probably my idea (which it wasn't). We were probably the only two suspects with the operating experience to actually accomplish the feat, so our silence on the matter only led to further suspicion. Many of our more memorable excursions had my fingerprints on them, which doesn't say a lot about what I used a good amount of my youth thinking about.

I always had pretty good organizational skills and it was probably not the best use of this talent. Part of this is the understanding of hierarchies. When people are in a group setting, there is always an order established of who listens, who leads, and who is to be entrusted with the honor of accepting a new member into the group. Teams are made up of individuals who have different status based on length of service, value, and the nebulous qualities that we encompass as leadership. When I was a brand new member of the team, I knew that whatever I might have thought about something was probably of little consequence to my teammates who were four years older. I was just a kid, and they were men. I kept my mouth shut and followed their lead.

After a year, I had earned the right to say a little but not much. The younger guys still looked above me for guidance and leadership. Fortunately, we had a Coach who was

121

a gifted leader and was always in control of any problems that might develop. I honestly can't remember a single fist-fight, other than ones between brothers that bubbled over from stuff that happened at home, occurring on our team in four years of running. And that is saying something when you think of how common fights are when there are a lot of strong willed individuals working together and constantly competing against each other.

Sometime in my junior year, our English teacher assigned us a Mark Twain story from our Literature book. Three of my teammates were in this class and a few days after the teacher gave us the assignment, Jude asked me if I had read the story. "The Man Who Corrupted Hadleyville" is a short story about one man's elaborate scheme to show the true greed and corruption of a town known for its forthrightness. I had read it over the weekend and had especially liked the story. I thought he was asking me so he could get me to tell him what it was about, assuming he probably had not read it.

"Yeah, I read it," I said.

"Sound like anybody you know," Jude asked.

I hesitated, running a list of names through my mind.

Denny was listening to us, and he looked at me through his squinty grin and said, "Sounds like somebody I know."

"What are you talking about?" I asked.

"What that guy did sounds like something *you* would do if you got mad at a town," Jude said.

"Hadley," Denny said as if the name just came to him.

"Hadley?" I was remembering the story of "The Man Who Corrupted Hadleyville" but it still wasn't registering with me what they were getting at.

"Hadley!" Jude added as if a decision had been made. The two of them seemed pleased with finally coming up with the answer to a long puzzled riddle.

Over the next week or so, the name caught on, as these two made a point of calling me "Hadley" at practice, when normally they would not have had a need to use a name in talking to me.

"So, uh, Hadley. Did you get some new shoes?"

Or, "Do you need a ride home after practice, Hadley?"

I didn't fight it too hard, as nickname etiquette doesn't allow for whining about the name you're called. The harder you resist, the stickier the name gets. I had been holding out for a good one-syllable nickname, like "Pre." Pre was someone we constantly were trying to imitate. Many of us had let our hair grow long, like Pre. We had taken to wearing a blue tee shirt under our yellow racing jerseys like the Oregon runners. We wore Nike racing spikes and Oregon waffles. Of course we knew that his nickname was a shortened version of his real name, but it was a great one.

I figured it would pass after a while. I was pretty proud of my given name and had avoided being called anything but what my mother and father named me.

I couldn't have been more wrong. Rather than go away, the name grew with variations that included first, middle, and several alternate surnames. Jude and Denny figured Mr. Hadley must have had at least one of each. Pete T. Hadley. Hadley T. Pete. P.T. Hadley. None of them or the several others who joined in to add their opinions or embellishments could seem to arrive at a consensus so they each settled on the one they liked best. To this day, one calls me Pete T. Hadley, another Hadley Pete, and several just refer to me as Hadley.

STEVE ADKISSON

Go Ask Alice
Just Another Day In Paradise
for Your Friendly Neighborhood Runner

-The Tatler, Volume I 1974

Talked with the loquacious Jude Baynum at a party Friday night. Sitting atop the porch roof and ably admiring the full moon with a dozen classmates as Bruce Springstein's "Born To Run" blared through the speakers set up on the window sill, I asked Jude how much he had been running. "I don't really count miles that close, but Steve says we get in seventy or eighty miles a week most the time. There's something going on with that guy. He don't say much, but he is ready for the season."

Steve, you may surmise, is fellow junior Steve Adkisson, the abstemious one, absent from the party?

"Yeah, that guy won't party in season," Jude reminded me. "He thinks the season started in June! Heh heh."

I've followed the running scene here at Juggerland since the beginning and I am not being facetious when I say I am sensing large things aflutter with the pack. Will the Regions cross-country teams remain obsequious to our top 7?

Anybody besides me noticed the hair?

Somebody say Sampson? Somebody say beware. Somebody say be aware.

There is something about apples pilfered from a tree near the end of a long run in September that makes them taste even better than the ones labeled "Fresh Picked" at the grocery store. This must be instinctive to human beings because I've watched dozens of kids deviate from the road course Coach set out for us and go straight through peoples' yards, into an orchard, grab the best apple within reach, and eat it on a dead run before they made it back to the locker room. No one had to show them how to do this so I know it is not a learned behavior.

In the not-too-distant past, people believed in feeding future generations from the land they lived on. This belief may have come as part of the Euro-American self reliance culture handed down through many generations. It survives in much of rural America and I am sure at least here in Kentucky it does. I am not even counting the farmers and ranchers. Probably ten in twenty suburban yards had large gardens and some sort of fruit trees that were immaculately cared for: pruned, mulched, fertilized, and generally left unguarded while in season. This last form of care is what leaves one with the impression that they wanted to feed future generations. When the apples were ripe in September they became at risk.

Maybe it is the low blood sugar levels that runners get near the end of a long run or the clearing of the nasal passages and the increased sense of smell this causes. Or perhaps it is that fruit still undergoing photosynthesis by being attached to the tree are just that much more delicious. Maybe it is the knack for being in tune with the nutrients the body needs. It's a question that probably won't be answered.

What the cross-country team needed at the end of a long run was Mr. Kramer's apples.

Mr. Kramer had one of the big five-acre spreads on Hulbert Avenue, which connected our town with a rural area west of the city limits. Of course our favorite runs went out this way. Our five-mile time trial course went straight out and back this very road. The Lonesome Valley, where wild ponies, creek crossings, and some of the steepest runable trails east of the Mississippi reside, was out this way. Several members of our team lived on streets that went off Hulbert. It was inevitable that Mr. Kramer would someday have to come and meet with Coach.

Most tales that adventurers (i.e. explorers, mountain climbers, and hunters) tell begin with "There I was . . ." Many of our tales begin with "These guys from Boone County . . ." Boone County High School is the nearest neighboring school to ours. We proudly wore the blue and gold of the Juggernauts and they had a powder blue and gray Colonel we always thought bore a strong resemblance to the Kentucky Fried Chicken logo. The rivalry that existed between the two schools was of the burn-their-mascot-in-effigy variety. I remember something about an outhouse being swapped back and forth, and a bell that weighed a hundred pounds being stolen and then stolen back. I think Mr. Kramer came to believe that all students at Boone County were juvenile delinquents and pathological apple thieves.

The day Mr. Kramer met coach was the day I learned I could never be a lawyer, (even though I would have a lot of practice as a public defender before my high school running career would be over, after somehow being notarized as the spokesman for the team's chicanery). What happened was some of the guys got greedy and weren't satisfied with just the one apple they could have eaten on the way back to school (and thereby destroying the evidence). No, somebody had to fill their shirt up and drag the whole team into the one place that loyal teammates least like to be dragged: a position of choosing between their own skin and that of a student from Boone County.

We were all back from the run, an easy six miler on the day after a meet. We were stretching under the big maple tree in front of school and coach was standing out in the parking lot a hundred feet away talking to a man in a red pickup truck. When coach turned and looked toward us, the man in the pickup pointed his finger and forty pairs of eyes went from the end of his finger to their own toes, worked their way skyward and eventually rolled back inside for a peek at the soul, just to see if it was sticking around for whatever happened next.

One thing you should know about Coach was that he would let you fry. He would fry you himself if he thought you needed frying. He had survived a tour of Vietnam, had made his living there driving a munitions truck - you know, the one with the big, giant letters E X P L O S I V E S painted on the side. At night and on weekends, he was a city policeman. So he didn't take lightly to breaking the law, which is what I think Mr. Kramer was explaining that some of those present had recently done.

Coach had body language I became expert at translating to the rest of the team. Because I had been born and spent the first years of my life in a part of western Kentucky where they still speak with slow southern drawls, I was assigned the duty of acting as interpreter of anybody else who spoke it. Being from Missouri, Coach's English wasn't always clear to some of my northern Kentucky born teammates. But you generally got the message he was intending to give by his gestures and tone.

I think what he was saying as he pounded the pavement with the soles of his shoes on his way back across the parking lot went something along these lines: "If I ever get my hands on the sneaking, thieving son of a b*&%# weasel behind this, I'm gonna tear his head off."

Of course this message didn't need translating, and everybody knew better than to be snickering and smiling. But just at this moment somebody's stretching efforts exceeded his body's natural tendency to keep all of its accumulated gases inside. Not only was the sound impressive – it really stunk. Coach had just heard the citizen's complaint and was

127

not, as you can imagine, in a humorous mood.

Coach knew I was good at a lot of things but that lying wasn't one of them. This must explain why he always chose me as the spokesperson for the group whenever accusations were made.

"Hadley," he said.

"Yes, sir?"

"Who stole the apples?"

A simple question, straight to the point. I stood up straight and pushed my hair back out of my face and tried to manage that look which shows both respect and perplexity. It was a look that through repeated practice and a fair amount of concentration, I was beginning to master. Coach loved us a lot and we knew how hard he worked at making us better runners, better students, and one day, hopefully, better adult human beings. As fiduciary of the entire team's future freedom to run the streets, I knew my answer had to be something Coach could swallow without gagging. I could only imagine the new parameters which would be put in place if he thought we were out vandalizing and stealing on his watch.

"Coach," I said. "We were all jogging back together, just cooling down, when these four guys from Boone County came out of the woods and cut through the orchard..."

I guess Coach quickly decided he didn't think he was going to get much else out of me or he knew already what had happened and he just didn't think this one was a big enough deal to turn it into a capital offense. He heard my story out but really wasn't buying it, I could tell.

"Hit the showers and get on home," he said as he shook his head and herded us off toward the locker room. He stood outside the door a minute rubbing his chin and I could tell he was trying to think of a way that he could satisfy everyone's interest. I am sure he had been threatened with the prospect of having the school administration's attention drawn to what "his boys" were doing. This would have been embarrassing as well as potentially career limiting for a young Coach in a sport that had very little support to begin with. He must have come to some conclusion but I was never really sure what it was. All I know is he started parking his truck in front of Mr. Kramer's house when we were due to pass by there on our way back from a run.

Later in the locker room while Coach was out smoothing over the situation, sweatshirts were quickly peeled off. Several sweaty powder blue and gray B.C.H.S. tee shirts were hastily put in gym bags to be taken home and stealthily laundered.

STEVE ADKISSON

"Whatever you do, don't do it halfway."

-Bob Beamon,
Olympic Long Jump Gold Medalist
who jumped 29' 2 ½" in 1968

Every great team has a "Go To" guy who is counted on to come through in the clutch, to get the big hit, score the winning basket, or rise above the pressure of a win or lose situation and perform above their own capabilities. Growing up I got to hang around a bunch of them. Only I always called him the "Go For" guy.

To say I grew up in a competitive environment is like saying that a pig only eats a peck of grit before he dies. My older brother Bill is a phenomenal athlete and from the earliest days of my existence I can remember trying to keep up with him. Among other athletic accomplishments, he earned a college scholarship to play baseball at a Division I School. He was my first "Go For" guy because I always wanted to hang out with him and do what he did. As we got a little older, I had to not only keep up with him but also with his friends who lived in the neighborhood. As a ten-year-old, I constantly found myself in baseball, basketball, and football games with kids a few years older. Several of these kids grew up to be extremely successful athletes including one NFL player, several college baseball players, and some National Championship caliber track and field athletes.

You don't, if you are just a going about the business of being a kid, know this will happen when you're ten years old so you are not intimidated. I was competing against kids who already had testosterone boiling in their blood when my body hadn't even contemplated developing.

130

Hardheaded as I was, I kept trying to beat them because, if for no other reason, I just hate to lose. I was never the kind of kid who cried when I lost, or threw equipment or tantrums. I hated losing, but I knew the only way not to lose was to just get better at what I was trying to do so I wouldn't lose any more. So I practiced. A lot.

We played all kinds of ball games. The teams were always chosen the old fashioned way where the two very best players (and everybody always knows who those were) would be the captains of the two teams. The remaining players would line up and the captains would alternate picking who they wanted to be on their teams. Depending on who all was there from the neighborhood, the choices were usually pretty predictable. We all grew to learn who could play and how well.

In the summers we would play sandlot baseball from early morning until lunchtime, hurry home for a peanut butter and jelly sandwich and a glass of milk then get back to the field and play all afternoon. Then we would go home, eat dinner, and go to baseball practice or the scheduled game with our organized teams. Most of us got pretty good at it too. The last two summers I played baseball when I was fourteen and fifteen, the team that Jude, John, and I were on played in the finals of the Greater Cincinnati Youth Baseball tournament, which were played at Riverfront Stadium where the Reds played.

In the fall we played tackle football. Without equipment. This was particularly dangerous for me since I can distinctly remember the day I broke 100 pounds - it was just before my junior year of high school. I don't remember bleeding much, but I do remember limping home a lot. I must have been born with a high pain tolerance. When I was thirteen, my mom took me to the doctor because I had this big knot on the front of my knee. They thought initially it was some kind of tumor because the x-ray showed a large mass where my patellar tendon attached to my kneecap. They took me in for exploratory surgery and removed a chunk of green glass, most likely from a Mountain Dew bottle. It must have gotten into the patellar tendon during one of the numerous bike wrecks I had a habit of having. I spent six weeks in a full leg cast which permanently atrophied all the muscles in my right leg.

In the winter we played basketball after school until suppertime. Then we would go back out and play in the fading light. When everyone else went in to get a bath and do their homework, I would shoot 100 free throws, or work on some new move I'd seen one of the older guys do. I particularly practiced the moves of Earl "The Pearl" Monroe whose smooth street ball moves were a couple of decades away from catching on in organized ball.

I fantasized about dunking. It is probably a good thing that I was too short to ever dunk. I truly believe if I could dunk a basketball I would have never run a step in my life. I would wake up in the morning and lace up my Chuck Taylors, stretch out a little bit, then go from one end of the basketball court to the other and dunk. When I got tired, I would rest a little bit, then dunk some more.

These older guys always had some especially slick behind-the-back in-your-face move that I was determined to master. One in particular was a tall wiry kid who could really jump and who was the first person I actually saw dunk a basketball. He was only fourteen years old. Larry had taken his dad's tape measure and drawn a take off point on the large concrete pad we played basketball on in his backyard and measured out 29' 2 ½". He told us he was going jump that far one day and meant it. You ever seen how far 29' 2 ½ " really is?

He did jump very far for a high school athlete but he

was the kind of guy who would later go on to complain that he was getting a cramp in his right quad because all the medals on his track letter sweater were causing him to walk crooked. He had two younger brothers and a neighborhood full of challengers who he was constantly squashing in any way he could think of. He would smack their shot back into their face and ask them if they would like any salt and pepper with their "basketball stew." He would taunt them until they would threaten to knock him out, which I never saw happen.

"Go for it!" was one of his favorite sayings. And Larry became the second "Go For" guy because he was the kind of athlete who was not satisfied with just beating you; he wanted to make sure you left mad after he beat you.

The prevalence of this phenomenon in modern sports is disheartening because it leaves too many young athletes with the impression that sport is about showing up your opponent rather than about striving to be the best you can be. There is definitely a place in sport for showmanship, and there is always an excitement in seeing some especially talented athlete do something spectacular. It's a very fine line between showing your stuff and showing off. Whenever someone on one of my teams crossed that line, they instantly became my "Go For" guy.

As my athletic inclinations took me away from ball sports into running, I brought this acquired competitiveness with me. As a young runner, I worked very hard to keep up with the older guys on my team. This is the way most of us improve over time in endurance sports, and it is what makes the growth and learning curve from age fourteen to eighteen so steep. It is not unusual to witness a distance runner's times come down by leaps and bounds as he simply goes through the grades. He begins as a gangly freshman with pimples and four years later can be considered a full-grown man. In between he endures a tremendous amount of growing up.

From my first day of cross-country practice as a freshman, I started up this learning curve, two steps at a time. It had to be steep because I actually thought it was called "cross-county" and that I was getting in shape for basketball.

Let's face it, it doesn't take any special skill to be a runner. Virtually any healthy person can run. Those of us attracted to cross-country were the kids who realized that we weren't going to play football in high school and who wanted to participate in a school sport, which isn't much of a qualification for excellence in any kind of athlete.

A few of the older runners had competed for several years and had developed a love for the sport, but had not really trained enough to improve. The fact that they were upper classmen, drove cars home from school, and seemed to actually enjoy running - all made a lasting impression on me. One in particular, Gary Graves, took me under his wing and became a "Go For" guy in the sense that I have tried to share my love for the sport with younger people in the same way he did with me.

The best kind of "Go For" guy is the one who is the best runner on the team. This creates the kind of challenge that makes everyone on the team better. From the very beginning, we had Matt who was a great runner and one of the nicest human beings I have ever known. The only problem was he wanted to be number one so intensely that he had to be number one at everything. Every training run, every workout, every repetition of an interval workout. It got to be annoying because we were all a little jealous, number one, that he could do it, and two, that he was so insistent about it. What bothered me was that, at a certain point, it wasn't doing anybody any good. An unspoken animosity developed which turned the "us" into a "him vs. us'"

We had a fairly standard workout we would do every few weeks. We were supposed to do 20 x 440 yards at seventy-five seconds on our "Trail of Tears" which was a loop of the front grounds of our school. The loop had two modest hills in it and was never measured that I know of, but if anything it was a little longer than a 440 on the track. Invariably there would begin to be a lot of racing in this workout, and the times would get down in the low 60's which would get pretty painful after a while. Still he would win every repeat.

Over the course of a couple years of this competition, a handful of us had improved enough by chasing Matt around town for hundreds of miles a month that we were actually beginning to challenge him a little. If he had a cold, or some slight injury, sometimes one or another of us would catch up with him, only to be outkicked at the end. It finally got to a point where something had to give, and inevitably what had to be done was to make him understand that some of the rest of us wanted to be first too.

Before one of these workouts when Matt was a senior, I sensed a growing aggravation among my teammates, and an unspoken decision was made to use the "Big Time Wrestling" equivalent of a tag team on him. Coach had challenged us to improve on our times from the earlier workout and we were supposed to be doing 20 x 440 yards at 72 seconds.

I took off like a jackrabbit and ran the first one in 63, finishing just behind Matt, but definitely had caused him to exert some effort. The rest of the pack came in at exactly 72 seconds and we had one minute to rest. Gerry took the next one and pushed it to 65 but still got beat while I cruised in with the pack. Then Johnny took a turn and pushed Matt through another 63, which wasn't an all out effort, but when you're looking at 17 more repeats with a minute rest, it is way too fast. Rested a little from the two slower repeats, I took off again on the fourth repetition, and when I got to 300 yards and was still ahead of Matt, I put my head down and kicked in like it was the Olympic open 400 meters.

I had finally beaten the Go For guy, even if it was just in a single interval in a single workout, and he came in winded and dragging his tongue on the ground. Of course he almost tripped over my tongue too, and we stood there and waited about 8 seconds for the rest of the team to finish in 72. I thought he might be getting a little ticked off about this, but he didn't let on like anything had happened. Instead, as we waited for the next repeat to begin, he seemed to regroup himself and, if anything, he looked more determined than ever as we started again. It was almost like he was saying, "OK, you want to play this game. Bring it on. Go for it." And we did.

It was like the movie *Jeremiah Johnson* where the Crow tribe kept sending out one warrior at a time to seek revenge on him. They kept popping up at random throwing everything imaginable at Jeremiah and he kept fighting it out. He took a spear here or a tomahawk there, but he always found a way to leave them lying in a pool of their own blood while he lived to fight another day.

Over the next half-hour, I believe I witnessed one of the greatest endurance performances I ever saw a high school runner complete. We continued to attack him one at a time and he stubbornly continued to race each of the attackers. No one else beat him that day and he must have averaged 64 seconds for the entire workout. He was so fit and so strong-willed that he would not allow any of us to beat him again.

JUGGERNAUTS

As anyone who has experienced interval training can attest, a really hard workout will drastically improve your performance, and this is exactly what happened with Matt. While we thought we were wearing him down, we were just making him stronger. But we were also making ourselves stronger too by pushing the limits of our own endurance in our efforts to beat him.

This is what being an endurance athlete is all about. Pushing, testing, expanding the limit of our own bodies. Finding what might have been impossible six months ago is doable today. By gradually pushing back the barriers, which are mostly in our minds, we are able to perform better than we could previously. The human body adapts to the stress put on it, and each time the mind learns that something better is possible. Like the natural competitiveness of thoroughbred horses, the entire group pushes each other towards achievements virtually impossible to achieve alone.

There is nothing that sticks to running shoes quite like the mud made up of hard packed Kentucky clay and two weeks worth of rain. These exact conditions existed for much of my high school running career as a new interstate highway I-275 was being excavated within easy running distance from our house. As the end of the excavation got further and further from my house over the years they built the highway, my endurance grew.

It also seemed there was rarely a long enough period of time when it didn't rain regularly enough for the clay to completely dry. The five-pound shoes this mud invariably provided me had to have an effect on my running. Besides increasing my leg strength, it also gained me the reputation in my neighborhood as the kid who had to hose off out in the yard before he was allowed in the house. My parents, to their credit, never really complained. I guess they figured there were quite a few worse things a teenage boy could be doing than going out for a ten mile run in the mud. What they never realized was how bad of an addiction it would become.

I started running when I was fourteen years old, and it only took about a week for me to get heavy duty into running in the mud. From the earliest days of organized running, both my coach and parents had warned me about staying safely off the busy roads, so I started running in areas where there was a wide shoulder beside the road. Gradually I started edging away from the road, slipping inch by inch into the grass and mud on the side.

One morning I went out for a four mile run. It had been raining all night and water puddled in the road and ditches beside it. A car came by and threw water from a six-inch deep puddle hard up against me. I jumped away as fast as I could, but somehow I ended up in the two-foot ditch beside the road, which had about a foot of water in it. I ran through the water in the ditch. At first I thought about getting out as quickly as I could, but after running about fifty feet further through the ditch, I felt something snap. I don't mean a tendon or a ligament in my leg. It was like a light went on, or a light went out, or something.

When I came to, a half-mile down the road, I was still running along in the ditch, kicking water and highstepping along when I saw a car coming down the road ahead of me. Somehow I felt self-conscious about letting someone see me in this condition so I got up beside the road again. After the car went by, I hopped down into the ditch again.

For a couple of years I would purposely go out to run in the rain just to get a chance to do this. By the time I got to the middle of my first cross-country season, I think even coach was getting the idea that maybe there was something a little off with me. Of course it didn't rain every day, and sometimes there would be hard dry dirt and dust for weeks, so for a long time I was able to hide my mud addiction from most people. I had the same coach for four years and he may have been the only person to have seen a pattern of behavior that would have been cause for alarm had I not functioned pretty normally when I wasn't running.

I was able to avoid any kind of intervention by explaining to Coach and my teammates that I was just running tangents, even when the tangent involved mucking fifty feet through six inches of mud, while the trail or course stayed high and dry and would have shaved ten or twenty seconds off my time.

One of the few constants in Kentucky weather is that after a drought there will be a monsoon season. The good thing about this is that as the cross-country season goes on from August through November, there is bound to be a prolonged period of rain and with the rain comes muddy cross-country courses. Some runners fear the sloppy course, but the nastier it is the bigger the smile on my face.

Every accomplished athlete has an easily identified breakthrough event that stands out as a big booster of the confidence and self-image that is vital to being a winner. Mine came on a rainy Saturday morning in the middle of September of my junior year. Northern Kentucky has one of the biggest and oldest invitational cross-country meets in the Midwest put on by Covington Catholic High School. Teams from several states and the best runners within Kentucky come together to measure their early season fitness.

I woke up that morning to pouring rain. Since the weather had been dry since the middle of July there would be a lot of runners for whom the soft and sloppy conditions would be a drastic change from what they were accustomed to running in for the last few months. I would have a chance to get a jump on the fastest guys with my finely honed special mud running skills.

I noticed as we warmed up that even my teammates were a little reluctant to get their shiny and relatively new spikes covered in the fresh mud. In that era, a new pair of spikes was such a rare and special occasion; we would gather at the home of the recipient of a new pair when they were first purchased to gawk and hold them in our hands and marvel at their beauty and lightness. A new outfit called Nike was putting out some decent shoes. I had saved up money and bought my own pair of the new Oregon Waffles, which like the name implies, had a sole surface fresh off Mrs. Bill Bowerman's waffle iron. I swear they had a smell like maple syrup when I first took them out of the box.

I had complete confidence in their gripping ability in the slick and sloppy mud of the course. I usually warmed up in my heavier training flats, but it was so nasty out that even I only wanted to have one pair of shoes to clean when I got home. I just put the Waffles on for my warmup run and figured they would be just as heavy as anybody else's shoes after the first 100 yards of the race anyway.

When the race started, I found myself near the front pack, which consisted of Jude and Matt, a couple Louisville area runners, and Billy Moormon from Daviess County. Over the first mile we sloshed along and gradually Moorman, my two teammates, and I managed to separate ourselves from the pack. Jude had really worked hard for a year to develop himself into a real contender, even if this was only the early part of his second cross-country season. Matt had been the best runner on our team for the previous two years. As one of three seniors on the team this year, and having run cross-country for four years, he was still the indisputable leader on our team.

140

JUGGERNAUTS

There is a saying in sport that somebody "owns you." This is exactly what Matt had done to me for the first two plus years of my running career. Even when he had bad days on the same day I was having a great day, he would find a way to beat me. He was a ferocious competitor.

There was a picture in the paper the next day that showed us rounding a tree which marked a turn in the middle of the course at the end of a long hill. Daviess County's Billy Moorman is in the lead and Jude is running right on my shoulder with concentration and determination written on his face. Matt is a half step behind, looking like he is still running uphill, tongue hanging out, grim.

I have just made the turn and have what from all outward appearances seems to be a smile on my face. I don't remember what could have caused me to laugh or find humor in something that I have always taken very seriously. Distance racing is always painful when it is done right and I can assure you that this far along in the race I was hurting too much to be laughing.

I'd have to believe the camera caught me at the very moment when I realized I actually had a chance to push through the barrier of confidence I needed to overcome if I was ever going to finally beat Matt. The fact that I actually enjoyed running hard through the mud was paying off in a way that was not only socially acceptable, it was happening in one of the biggest races of the year.

Right after we turned the corner, Jude accelerated and I went with him. We passed Moorman – Jude on one side and me on the other. Jude tapped his shoulder and said, "Hey bub, mind if we run up here with you for a while?" This was just like Jude, who developed friendships with many of our competitors because of his gregarious nature. He didn't do this to provoke or belittle the competition; he just couldn't help it.

141

I continued to push the pace and while the others slipped around the trickier spots I seemed to float over the mud keeping my momentum up through the turns and up-hill sections of the course.

I crossed the finish line in first place in a cross-country race for the second time in my life, but this time it was against the best competition available to me. My two teammates were hard on my heals, and our team gave out what Coach called an old fashioned Kentucky butt-whuppin to all-comers that day, placing our first five run-ners in the top ten. Steve Nienaber had probably one of his best races ever, and my brother John was gaining confi-dence as he finished closer and closer to the front. All of us were excited, even Matt, who from that day forward was an even better friend than before. Each of us recognized our hard work was making all of us better, that the entire team was extremely fit. On any given day, somebody was going to have an edge and knowing this made our whole team stronger by having so many fierce competitors to train with and to suit up with on race day knowing we were all in this together.

Matt still competed hard with me after that, but because of a combination of injuries he had and the increased confi-dence I had gained, he did not beat me in another cross country race. For the next two years I would race in flats or spikes on the dry fast courses around Kentucky, but when-ever the course was muddy, I'd pull those Oregon waffles out of my bag and slap the soles together and let the previ-ous run's dried-up mud splatter over the grass. I'd already put on my smile.

JUGGERNAUTS

Steve Adkisson Gets A Hug From Mom
Mary Ann Adkisson can't contain her enthusiasm after her son's victory

You don't need to know much about my mom to see
she was proud of her son.
Covington Catholic Invitational 1974.
Kentucky Post.

After winning the Covington Catholic Invitational meet
against many of the best teams in the state, we had a great
week of practice. We were extremely motivated and were
enjoying the newspaper articles claiming us as the team to
beat.

Sunday, September 15, 1974 The Cincinnati Enquirer
At Covington Catholic Invitational
It Looks Easy For Lloyd Harriers

By Herb Whitney
Enquirer Sports Reporter

STEVE ADKISSON

The Erlanger-Lloyd cross-country team went about its business of winning with such precision Saturday that several of the coaches watching were left in a state of shock.

Specifically, Mike Daley's Lloyd runners ran away with the small-school varsity race in the seventh annual Covington Catholic Invitational at Camp Marydale. Lloyd posted an impressive 21 points to leave perennial power Daviess County, which came in second, far back with 81 points. Defending state Class A champion West Hardin was third with 90.

Lloyd put five runners in the top eight. Junior Steve Adkisson came in first, cruising over the two-mile layout in 10 minutes and 5 seconds. Lloyd teammate Jude Baynum was second in 10:11, while Matt Huff placed fourth, John Adkisson sixth and Steve Nienaber eighth.

"This may be the best race I've ever seen my kids run," said beaming Lloyd coach Mike Daley after the rout. "It's taken three years to get where we are. Three years of hard work and dedication. These kids all work on their own – before school, after school, whenever they can. They deserve a lot of credit." . . .

JUGGERNAUTS

"Anger is implanted in us as sort of a sting, to make us gnash with our teeth against the devil, to make us vehement against him, not to set us in array against each other."

-Richard Savage
English poet and satirist

As the season went along, Jude obtained a lucky red hat and he wore it with great effectiveness the entire year. Dave Wottle won the 1972 Olympic 800 meters wearing a golf hat and made famous the hat-on-a-distance-runner phenomenon. There were several uniform violation discussions with officials that took place before meets when some of the opposing coaches would try to make a big deal out of it. Coach Daley would say "Come on coach, you don't think that hat gives a kid that much of an advantage do you? If it did, I'd just make it a standard issue part of our uniform and put them on the whole team!" He would chuckle and wag his head. That was usually the end of it and Jude got to wear his hat.

Coached stayed quiet on the issue of our pre-ordained success at winning the State Championship, but I could tell he was excited about our chances. He set up some very challenging workouts for us and then set back and watched us thrash each other at practice all week.

My logbook shows that we did a long hill workout on Monday, then had a dual meet the next day. After the meet, several of us went for a five-mile run. On Wednesday, we did 8 x 660 and then 6 x 330, all fast with short rest intervals in between. Thursday was an easy eight mile road run and then Friday, we backed off and did just four miles. We ran four miles each morning.

Even though this was a typical mid-season week for us,

I think Coach may have purposely set the training load high so that we would be fatigued by the time the race came on Saturday. He may have known that we still had some lessons to learn, but he let us enjoy our newfound confidence.

Down in Owensboro, Kentucky, the coach and runners of Owensboro High School must have been sticking voodoo pins into the pictures of us that had accompanied the articles about our victory in the Covington Catholic Invitational. Owensboro had not competed in the race, so they had sought out information about it through the newspapers. The writers quoted several local coaches who had declared us the next state champions by virtue of our performance in this early season meet. The only problem with this, from their point of view, was that the writers were apparently counting them out of the picture. Owensboro had won the State Championship four consecutive years and had perennial contenders for the individual title in recent years thanks to an excellent coach and some very dedicated runners. They had several seniors on their team who had placed high in the previous year's championship as juniors. Johnny Jones, their number one runner, was being recruited by Western Kentucky University, which already had Nick Rose, Tony Staynings, and several other Olympic caliber distance runners attending.

One week after our team's first big win of the season, we drove to Owensboro to compete in the Owensboro Invitational. They were waiting for us.

Owensboro's team uniform was a red and white vertically striped jersey and shorts. Their runners were hard to miss when you were looking out over a cross-country course. Up close they had a tendency to mesmerize you if you were running right behind one of their runners. Coach had given us more thorough race strategy than usual before this race, instructing us to be aware of the Owensboro runners and to remember that every point would be crucial to a team victory. He spoke especially to our 5, 6, and 7 runners, indicating that picking off just one of the red and white "candy stripers" might be the difference in the race.

Jones was only a little taller than me and had long curly hair. He had won the State Championship the previous year so we had an immense amount of respect for him even though our team seldom ever raced against a rival team on the other side of the state. When the race began, our entire team pushed to the front of the pack and was instantly infiltrated by the entire Owensboro team, with Jones surging up beside us. We were so accustomed to running together in training every day that it felt strange to have so many others mingling with us as we hammered along.

After about a half mile, I glanced around to see which of my teammates were still in the lead pack, and saw only Jude and Matt. The rest had fallen back. They would tell me later that the pace was just way too fast, and I agreed with them, but at the time I was just doing my best to hang on and stay relaxed.

Going at what was an insanely fast pace this early in a race, I was surprised to hear the two Owensboro runners beside me engaged in conversation. Away from the crowds at the starting line, the only sounds you usually hear in a race are the whispers of running shorts rubbing back and forth as you stride and the soft impact sounds of spikes hitting the ground. Later in a race, I would listen to the breathing of a competitor and judge how he was feeling from the sounds he was making.

One of the common ways Coach would instruct us to run on easy days was to run no faster than you could carry on a conversation. If you are running hard, you have to breathe at a rate that is too fast to be able to talk. This had been ingrained in us as a way to measure exertion on a run. All our "easy" workouts were supposed to be run at a conversational pace.

To be capable of speech at this pace and this far into the race meant that they were still nowhere near the limits of their endurance and this added to my concerns about being able to keep up. It bothered me, number one that they could do this, and number two, that they seemed to be intentionally letting us know they could do it.

We came through the first mile at 4:43 and there was still a lead pack of 6 of us. Jude was barely hanging on and Jones had eased to the front, bringing another of the Owensboro runners with him. Billy Moorman from Davies County High School and one from Paducah were also with us.

After the mile mark, we came back around to the finish line where the spectators were gathered. Many in the crowd screamed enthusiastically for the Owensboro runners as we passed by and started back around for another lap. Once away from the crowd, the two Owensboro runners accelerated slightly and then looked around to see if any of us would follow. I made a push to catch back up, but my legs were just dead. I was close enough to hear them talking but I couldn't make out what they were saying. Jones looked back again and then just took off like he had been jogging a warmup lap the first time around. I ran as hard as my body would let me, but as it turned out, I watched the back of those two red and white striped jerseys for the rest of the race. As we came into the finishing chute, the tall Davies County runner sprinted by me and I was helpless to respond.

The course, as it turned out, was 2.4 miles, which was longer than usual for a Kentucky high school race. While that extra .4 of a mile doesn't sound like much, those extra two minutes of racing came as a shock to most of us, adding to the suffering. After the week of hard workouts, our bodies were worn out and we ended up a distant second place to Owensboro. Several of my teammates were so spent when they finished that they collapsed in the finish chute, which was a big no-no for us. Part of our "Don't Be A Wussy" motto included the assumption that if you could run two miles at full speed you could walk a couple hundred more yards to your car when you were finished. In fact, it became a whole separate contest to see who could appear the freshest immediately upon finishing a race, which was an amusing testament to the willpower of the runners on our team. The finish chute of this race resembled the "March of the Zombies" as my blue and gold clad teammates stumbled through and took their finish cards to where coach was waiting to collect them.

It was a long ride home. After the previous week's jubilation, we had encountered a challenge we could not match. No one made excuses, but instead each of us was genuinely upset with ourselves for having let the team down. My 4th place finish individually was not good enough for me and each one of my teammates also expected more from their efforts.

When Coach dropped us off at school later that afternoon, he told us to take Sunday completely off – no running. He hadn't said too much to us about the race, letting it all soak in, as we drove home. He knew we were disappointed but in a way, I think he also had hoped something like this would happen to us early in the season. He did not want us to get overconfident or underestimate the competition we would have the rest of the season.

Not only did we learn humility by our defeat at Owensboro, but also we were re-inspired to train even harder so we could improve. All of us knew that if we were going to get better, something had to change. We could not expect to perform at the level we had at Owensboro and accomplish our goal of becoming State Champions.

John Adkisson and Matt Huff (closest to camera) dueling it out at home course 1974.
Spectator Yearbook photo.

The following month of training was the most brutal stretch of any of my high school seasons. Our entire team was motivated like never before. Matt, Steve, and Dave, as seniors, knew this was their last opportunity to compete in a sport they loved. Jude and I were also aware that this was their last season with us and, along with our brothers John and Gerry, we wanted to make the most of our abilities so we could all share in our accomplishments.

After our disappointing loss, I went on a ten meet winning streak. Jude, Matt, and I would take off ahead of the field and run together for a mile or so. We learned from the Owensboro runners how disruptive to a competitor's concentration talking amongst ourselves could be. Jude had come up beside me in the first race after Owensboro and calmly asked "How you doing, Hadley?"

I looked over at him and he was smiling, knowing how I had whined that "those two Owensboro guys not only ran away from me, but were telling each other fairy tales while they did it." My first instinct was to reach over and punch him. But when I saw he had the "just messing with you" smile on his face, I backed off of that.

"Not bad. You?" I replied and smiled at the thought that we were probably making the other team's runners as ticked at us as we had been at the Owensboro runners.

In the early part of these races while we were still able to converse, somebody would say something inane just to initiate a discussion. The Word of The Day would find its way into the couple of sentences or questions spoken during the first half mile or so of the race. It was never me, but it got to where my teammates knew this riled me so they kept at it mercilessly. This became a subtle reminder to us of how we had gotten a butt whuppin a few weeks back and it always fired me up. It seldom took more than a minute of hearing conversations in the early part of a race before the three of us would proceed to try to run each other into the ground. We were friends, but we were also ruthless competitors. Our racing strategy was pretty simple: go as hard as you can for as long as you can. With the fitness I had from all the hard training I had done in the previous year, I was physically stronger and was able to hold the fast pace and pull away over the last half-mile. Some coaches believe there is no training like racing, and likewise that it takes maybe a dozen races in a season to really get to the highest level of fitness. I never won by more than five or ten seconds, so no race was easy. In fact, each successive race seemed harder than the previous. The difference between us was the confidence I had in my fitness.

I lost one race to a rival named Rod Cook from Franklin County High School at their invitational held on the Saturday after our Homecoming Football Game and the dance which followed. Jude's girlfriend and my girlfriend were both seniors and the four of us had gone together to the homecoming dance and ended up staying up much later than we should have. Not getting enough rest might have been a reason for losing, but it was an unacceptable excuse. It was another of the lessons to me that there are sacrifices a runner has to make to get the most out of his talents and training.

I had beaten Rod Cook by twenty seconds earlier in the season and was embarrassed to lose to him, even though I finished ahead of my two teammates who I considered my fiercest competition. With only a couple of weeks left before the Regional Championship, I got back to work to make sure I was in the best shape possible for the remainder of the season.

We ran several intense team workouts on the "trail of tears" in front of school. An aerial photographer had taken a picture of the school about this time of year and a 3' x 4' black and white print was hung in the entrance hallway of the school. You could plainly make out the brown dirt path that our spikes had worn in to the ground, even from 3,000 feet above it.

We had two small home meets before the Regional and I won these, but only by the slightest of leads over my two teammates. We were extremely fit and these races must have been brutal for our competition. Six times during the year, we scored a perfect fifteen points as our first five runners finished ahead of the opponents' first runner. Our 4, 5, 6 and 7 runners were only twenty to thirty seconds slower than I was and I was setting course records on many of the courses in Northern Kentucky. We were all enjoying good health and coming to our peak of fitness at the end of the season.

Home meet 1974. Steve Nienaber closest to camera.
Jude in his lucky red hat.
Steve Adkisson getting out to an early lead

STEVE ADKISSON

"In a race all the runners run, but only one receives
the prize. So run that you may obtain it."

-Corinthians 9:24

In the week leading up to the Regional Meet, there were
articles in the paper almost every day. Coach had developed
relationships with several of the local sportswriters and they
would call him at home in the evening to gather information
for their stories. He had a way of phrasing the facts in such
a way as to allow the writers to extract a balanced story.

Coach would never come right out and say, "I think we
won't have any trouble in repeating as Regional Champions." What he would say was: "Highlands and Covington
Catholic have been closing the gap on us all season.
Holmes has been surprising a lot of teams here in the last
month. We've struggled in the bigger meets this year like
Owensboro and Harrison County. I know our boys are as
ready as they can be for the race Saturday, but there are always things that happen in a race that you can't predict."

What he had done was point the writer toward finding
out more about how the Highlands and Covington Catholic
and Holmes teams had done against us. These teams were
our fiercest competition and we had developed a strategy of
quietly harboring the highest contempt for any individual or
team who was a threat to us.

The writer would then pursue this information by
speaking with the other teams' coaches and of course
would include quotes from them in the printed article. Invariably, the coaches would praise their teams and give a
listing of their top kids – the names of whom we had already placed at the top of our shitlist.

After school each day, somebody would bring articles

154

cut out from their family's morning paper and would read these out loud while we changed into our running clothes and stretched. Coach always waited for us out in front of the school so we had the locker room pretty much to ourselves. It was probably best that he not hear the ensuing swearing and laughing and name calling that went on as the guys on the team gave their opinions of the runners talked about in the newspaper articles. We knew Coach would not condone this attitude, but among ourselves, we were free to express how we really felt.

I usually kept my mouth shut out of humility, but I didn't do anything to discourage my teammates from saying what they wanted. It was mostly meant in good fun, but there were always a few names they could bring up that would light a fire under me. Just the mention of Johnny Jones or Rod Cook was enough to get my heart rate up. I was counting down the days until I could race them again. Hearing all of this just before going out the door to practice most certainly made for highly motivated practices.

Momentum is one of those things that sometimes when you have it, you don't really appreciate it like you should. A lot of times you are not even aware you have it until long after it has been lost. The momentum I developed during the middle part of the season was one of those things hypnotists might try to get you to believe if they wanted you to imagine being invincible. This was pretty much how things had gone for me. I managed to avoid injuries, not get any major illness, and had the psychological edge of knowing I could run hard enough to exhaust my competition in the middle of a race.

Steve Prefontaine had already emerged as America's top middle distance runner and there wasn't a runner around who hadn't read his statements about a race being

155

the place to find out who had the most guts. When I lined up on a starting line and looked up and down the line, I had no fear of anyone. My hardest efforts a lot of times were at practice where my teammates and I would thrash each other in trying to get our interval times down. I did not have much confidence in my finishing speed, but I had developed a race strategy that "put crap in their legs" as Pre had said. We used to joke about our team's simple race plan: "Go out hard, run as fast as you can in the middle, then kick like hell at the end." That was exactly my plan.

Through the season, this plan had served me well. I was consistently able to push hard from the beginning and eventually spread out the field to just a few competitors. Usually right after the halfway point I would put in another surge and get enough of a lead to discourage a competitor from even trying to outsprint me at the end. It was a good thing too because most of the time, I was wobbling back and forth down the last 100 yards totally exhausted from the effort I had put out. If anyone was still with me they would have managed to kick past me at the end because I was slowing down.

Our Regional Meet was held on the same course in 1974 as it had been in my previous two cross country seasons. One Saturday a year, the Highland Country Club in Campbell County would ask their golfers to wait until 11:00 to schedule tee times and the Region would hold one race for all the eligible schools. The course was a simple one mile loop consisting of a long downhill start, several nasty steep hills in the middle, and then finished on the same long uphill where we started. We raced two laps. The course was accurately measured and was the benchmark of courses because the exact same course could be easily marked from year to year. The turns were large trees that had been there a hundred years. To my knowledge, this course had been the Regional course for thirty years. The times recorded could be measured from year to year and you would know how your performance compared to the previous year as well as to the long list of great runners who had raced on the course.

The winning time the year before had been 9:40 by my teammate Matt. He had battled the best in the Region and beaten out several outstanding rivals and gutted out a furious kick to lead our team to its first Regional Championship. We knew his great ability and competitive instincts would drive him to run faster this year on the same course. What we didn't know was by how much or what place a 9:40 two mile would get him.

Jude and I had been great friends for nearly a decade and even though we were both ferocious competitors, there were only a couple of times when our competitiveness overcame our friendship. This race was one of them.

I do not even remember what initiated what could only be described as "bad blood" between us leading up to the race. I know we had some hard times at my house where racing served as a release of pent up anger and frustration. I also know Jude went through some of the same things with the same kind of attitude. We didn't punch walls or yell; we laced up the spikes and went to work trying to make the other runners' hearts explode. It may have been only that each of us was driven to win and each of us had worked extremely hard to reach a certain peak level of fitness which has only one way to be dealt with: a great release of energy concentrated into our efforts to run fast.

Whatever the reason, the result was we set out that day to run each other into the ground. Race day was very cold, with a gusty wind. We did a longer warm-up than usual and kept our sweats on until just before being called to the starting line. Right as the gun went off, we both tore out into the front of the pack and left it chasing us down the long straightway of the golf course. We never looked back. Instead we both knew the only task at hand was to keep pushing the pace until one or the other of us couldn't keep up any longer.

Through the first lap, we ran side by side, hammering away at a pace that seemed fast but not so fast that either of us was suffering. Neither of us spoke or even looked over at each other, both focused on the small space of grass a few yards ahead of us.

There wasn't a clock at the mile marker, but coach was there calling out our times. We came through halfway in 4:43, on pace for a sub 9:30.

Maybe it was hearing this mile split and still feeling under control. Maybe it was a new rush of inspiration in seeing and hearing all the spectators who had come out to watch this meet and who were gathered at the start / finish line. Most likely, it was that both of us felt these exact same things and the fitness to do something with it. We started into the second and final lap even faster than we had run the first. Jude gained a few strides on me and this gave me a new burst of competitive fire. I responded and caught right back up as we continued to increase the pace going back down the long hill.

There is something about downhill running which doesn't appeal to me and it may be because sometimes late in a hard run, leaning to compensate for the angle of foot placement on a downgrade causes your stomach muscles to engage in a way that can give you a side stitch. Jude was too proud to make any excuses, but I have to believe that as we got to the bottom of this long downhill section, he got a stitch or some sudden new pain because as we started back uphill, he noticeably slowed down. I powered up the hill expecting him to catch right back up, but when I didn't hear him coming I pushed harder to try to open up as much of a gap as I could. I knew Jude had a better finishing kick than me and I needed to put some distance between us before we got to the finishing straightaway because I knew he would be coming back.

Steve Adkisson 1974 Regional at Highland Country Club.
Author collection. Photographer unknown

I can honestly say, and the recorded times would show that I ran faster in other races since then, but I never ran *harder* in a high school meet than I did over this last mile. I pushed the next few rolling hills as hard as I could knowing there was a gradual downhill between the 1 ½ mile and the uphill finish which was about 400 yards long. When I reached the bottom of this downhill section and took a slight left hand turn, I looked up the hill and could see the flags marking the finish chute as well as the 300 or so spectators lined out into a gauntlet extension of the chevron shaped finish chute.

I resisted every curious bone in my body to turn and take a peek to see where Jude was. Instead, I just put my head down and went all out for the finish. My legs were gaining weight with every step, but still I was moving very well. The back of my head, my shoulders and upper arms were numb and tingling from the exertion over this last mile. My vision became fuzzy on the edges. Time slowed down to nearly geologic as far as my perception of it was concerned.

The spectators were yelling encouragement but I could not make out any of the words or recognize any of the voices. It was just external white noise to the virtual symphony of activity going on in my own head and body. I concentrated on keeping my form, lifting my knees, maintaining my arm action, and driving toward the finish like a sprinter. Somewhere in this last ten seconds, I felt an unexplained power enter my body and lift all of the heaviness from my legs and I regained a bounce and strength I had never experienced at the end of hard race effort. My mind cleared and with this clarity I could see, hear, and feel everything going on around me. Right as I got near the end, I could tell from the eyes and shouts of the spectators that someone was right behind me. It could only be Jude and again I had to have the big discussion with myself about not looking back. Somehow I managed it, and finished in 9:18 with Jude closing hard right behind me in 9:19.

In keeping with The Code, I had to use every bit of will power in my body to stand up straight, smile, and look like I'd just finished an easy jog around the block. I came through the end of the chute and took my finish card. I turned and congratulated Jude while we both watched way down the hill for the rest of our teammates to finish.

Now that the race was over, it was like there was nothing wrong. Jude had that same genuine smile and said "Way to go Hadley!" We shook hands and jogged back around the spectators to get in the front of the gauntlet to encourage our teammates who quickly came across in great races of their own. Matt, John, Gerry, Steve, and Dave each ran their best race so far and we ended up winning decisively.

The main difference between this year and the year before was that we didn't really even celebrate winning the Regional Meet. Later that evening, we had a bonfire party at Jeff's farm but we mostly just sat around quietly watching the fire. I was even more subdued than usual and when Jude asked me if I was alright, I took a look around to make sure there was no one present who would misunderstand what I was about to say.

The experience I had at the end of the race had left me both totally amazed and halfway afraid. In the mental state of running at the extreme edge of what was possible for me, I had what I think most people would call a vision. At first I sloughed it off as one of those goofy aspects of my peculiar way of thinking, but as the day went on the images and feeling kept popping back into my mind.

"I think I saw God today," I whispered. I didn't raise my eyes from the fire but I could feel the mutual "What the. . .?" they were thinking.

After an uncomfortably long pause, Gerry said "Well, so what's so bad about that?" and everybody, including me, laughed. Nothing further was ever said about this and it was one of those things that later on I sort of wished I'd kept to myself because it really is a strange and difficult experience to explain. So it must have been as difficult to understand for anyone else as it was for me to try to fathom. All I can say about it is that I went to a place spiritually and mentally that I know changed me, and maybe even made me afraid to want to go back to.

We knew from the year before that there was a bigger goal for the team to strive for and this was just a stepping stone in that direction. Coach had even planned our training for the week before the Regional so we were not completely tapered or rested for this race. We had done some very hard workouts right up to Thursday before the Region and psychologically, we believed this gave us a boost to know we could even be better prepared with a little more rest when the State Meet came around the following weekend.

Our final training week went like this:

October 20 30 minutes fartlek. Nite: 15 min easy jog
October 21 Warmup; 20 x 440 at 70-72 (fastest 56)
  warmdown
October 22 Warmup; 24 x 220 fast striding; 2 miles
  warmdown
October 23 Warmup; 35 x 110 fast striding; Nite 3
  miles easy
October 24 30 minutes easy jogging
October 25 2 miles easy

JUGGERNAUTS

What started out to be the perfect season was coming to its conclusion and this final week of preparation had brought the team together in a way that was somehow both euphoric and melancholic at the same time. We knew something exciting and immensely challenging was set out in front of us, but we also knew this was the end in some ways to something which had been a constant in our lives for several years. Three of my best friends and teammates would be running their very last cross-country meet and as the week went by, this seemed to be the prevailing thought in our minds. We spent a lot of time talking about "old times" even though I was just sixteen years old. I had been educated and protected by Matt Huff and Steve Nienaber over the last three seasons, while Dave Crump had emerged as one of the hardest workers on the team to move up to become our number 7 runner. Our last few days of running together had become more or less a time to look back and see how far we had come.

Naturally my brother John and I, as well as the Baynums, had a bond that only brothers can have, but I know there is also a brotherhood which extends beyond blood to those who have worked hard over a long period of time for a common cause, who have stood beside each other through failures and successes. We knew each other well enough to know not only what skeletons were in each other's closets, but the combinations to the locks on the closet door. Our cause was in site, and what was surprising to me was that we were almost reluctant to reach out and grasp it.

The 1974 State Meet was held at a different venue than the previous year's, where the course had been virtually flat. While few courses we ran were as challenging as the hilly courses in Northern Kentucky, the Seneca Park course in Louisville did have some hills to challenge the runners.

Each of us had a different perspective of how well the course helped or hurt our chances.

In any race there is a story for every competitor. Each runner has his own goals and expectations, most of which have to do with how well he has performed against the known competition: "I know I can beat this guy or that guy because I have beaten them in the past." Only a very small number of competitors actually believe they can win, and the rest are content to know they will do the very best they can possibly do. Each runner goes to the line with his own state of readiness, his own internal motivation, and the outcome is decided by a combination of so many variables that it is rare to predict the exact outcome of any race. There are virtually an infinite number of factors which determine how an athlete will perform. Everything from the effectiveness of prolonged training, or illnesses caused by microscopic viruses, to the amount and quality of sleep two days before the race, the food you've eaten, the amount of warm-up miles it takes to get the body at its optimum performance level, the confidence absorbed from a coach's last piece of advice before heading to the starting line. So many things have to go right for an athlete to be "on" that it is no wonder there are so many excuses given when an athlete doesn't win.

I hate excuses. I try never to make them. My memory of running in the 1974 State Meet consists of struggling to just keep up with the front end of the pack. After having such a successful season, I had set my expectations very high for this particular day and for whatever reason, I just didn't have "it." Even though I finished third and our team won the State Championship, I had set my sights on winning the individual title and I was extremely disappointed.

Jude had an exceptional day and finish second to Johnny Jones. The Louisville paper told the story from a

JUGGERNAUTS

perspective that I hadn't realized until I read the article several days after the race:

THE COURIER-JOURNAL & TIMES,
SUNDAY, OCTOBER 27, 1974

Opposing coach's remark spurs Jones to 2nd AA title

By Roger Nesbit
Courier-Journal & Times Staff Writer

Owensboro's Johnny Jones, fired up because of a statement made by Erlanger Lloyd coach Bill Dailey (sic), yesterday won his second State Class AA individual cross-country title. Dailey got the last laugh, though, as Lloyd took the team title at Louisville's Seneca Park.

Dailey had commented in a previous article in The Courier-Journal that he thought two of his runners, Jude Baynum and Steve Adkisson, would dethrone the champ. But Jones had other notions.

"That comment made me mad," the short, curly-haired Jones said afterwards. "I really wanted to prove something today. This was my best race ever." He was clocked in 9:41.7 for the two-mile course.

Although Baynum (9:50) and Adkisson (9:55) finished right behind Jones, it was Bill Moorman of Daviess County that gave the Owensboro senior his stiffest competition through most of the race.

For about a mile and a half of the two-mile race, Moorman and Jones ran head-and-head. But Jones put on a strong finish up a slight hill in the final 700 yards and pulled away from everyone to win by approximately 30 yards.

165

STEVE ADKISSON

"This is the toughest course that I've run on," Jones commented. "But I like those hills. I had a good start and a great finish." Jones time of 9:29.4 in the state meet at Collings Estate last year is still the AA record.

"I thought Johnny ran a better race in the regional," said Owensboro coach Mike McKay. "I don't know why he thinks it's a hard course – I think it is one of the easier courses I've seen."

Daviess County's Moorman was not bitter about his loss. "Those hills hurt me," the junior said. "I thought Jones would win though. He's a great runner." Moorman's time was 9:56.

Lloyd's Baynum said "I thought me and Steve (Adkisson) would finish one and two. I like these hills."

Adkisson, who edged Moorman by a yard for third, said "this course is too flat. It was not my best race but Jones was great. I think he's the best runner in the state."

With Baynum getting second, Adkisson third, and Matt Huff sixth, Lloyd managed to coast past Lexington Tates Creek 55-73 for the team title. Jerry (sic) Baynum, a freshman, finished 33rd to aid the Lloyd cause. Tates Creek placed four runners in the top 14 but it was not enough to prevent Lloyd from gaining the title from defending champ Owensboro.

Owensboro had only one other runner, Mitch Settle, in the top 25 and had to settle for third with 100 points.

Jones got off to a smooth start and ran at the head with Moorman and three other runners for the first half mile. Then the pair pulled into a 10-yard lead over the pack and ran head-and-head for almost a mile.

But the final half mile of the course rises up a slope of about five degrees. Here Moorman started to falter while Jones kept his pace. Quickly Baynum shot by Moorman and soon afterwards Adkisson pulled abreast of the Daviess

166

County runner.

Baynum was not able to threaten Jones, who had a large lead, and the big battle was for third from Adkisson winning by a small margin. Then came Gary Tilman of Tates Creek with Huff on his heels at the finish.

Rod Cook of Franklin County was 20 yards further back and then Roger Vold of Christian County nipped both Allen Harvey and Ken Sagan of Tates Creek at the wire for eighth.

Lloyd has a bright future in that the state champs will lose only Huff to graduation. And with Jones departing from the high school ranks after this school year, Baynum and Adkisson could be fighting each other for the title next year.

Jones' win, contrary to last year when he surprised people, was expected by most of the crowd. But the tiny ball of fire was out to convince EVERYONE – especially the Lloyd coach – that he's tops. And that he did.

Matt Huff, Steve Adkisson, Dave Crump, Mike Daley,
Steve Nienaber, Jude Baynum, John Adkisson –
my guess is Gerry Baynum had detention.
Spectator Yearbook photo.

But the real story of our team's victory appeared a week later in our local paper.

As the week went by and our team was honored at a school pep rally, were guests on a local radio sports show, and were taken to the best steak house in the area for a celebratory dinner, each of my teammates had a chance to be given their due credit for the contribution they made in helping our team. It wasn't until I read this story that the thrill of victory finally sank in for me. It made me ashamed for having pouted over my disappointment and being so focused on what I had perceived as my failure to perform up to my own selfish expectation.

Steve Nienaber had become one of my best friends and biggest supporters. He had been on the team when I first started running and had consistently offered every encouragement and the benefit of his wisdom when I knew very little about being a runner. He trained as hard as or harder than any of us. He was always the first to congratulate and give a pat on the back or a kick in the butt to anyone on the team who needed it. Steve was probably the least talented of any of the varsity runners but the most willing to give everything he had to give to be our consistent fourth or fifth scoring runner.

Because of his contribution, our team had fought its way to the top of the competitive heap and I had been so caught up in my own disappointment that I had nearly overlooked one of the gutsiest performances any one of us had ever accomplished.

JUGGERNAUTS

THE KENTUCKY ENQUIRER
Sunday, November 5, 1974

Lloyd Spirit Behind Big State Title Win
Cross County (sic) Victory Effort

Steve Nienaber awoke with an upset stomach at 3 o'clock on a Saturday morning. He vomited and went back to sleep.

He dreamed he was running for Erlanger Lloyd High School in the state Class AA cross-country meet in Louisville. He woke again abruptly. The dream didn't say how his team or he had done in the race. It ended, as it had begun, in mystery.

"I thought the meet was all over and none of us would ever know how we had done," said Nienaber, recalling those annoying moments of eight days ago. "I just lay in my bed wondering how we had done. It scared me. When I finally realized it had all been a nightmare I felt better. I felt like someone who's been given another chance, a new life. We could go down to Louisville and still win it all, I thought."

Nienaber had another upset stomach before he and his Lloyd teammates boarded a school station wagon to go to Louisville. On the trip down he felt fine.

"I was weak from the virus I had, but I thought I could put it out of my mind," he said. "I thought I could psyche myself up. It was my last race for the school, and I didn't want to let anyone down."

Soon after the two-mile race started, however, Nienaber knew he'd have to struggle just to finish.

"After 200 yards I felt tired," he said. "I knew I wouldn't be able to help the team the way I should. Actually, the first mile went pretty well. I stayed up in the race

169

all right. But the second mile I got dizzy and didn't know where I was.

"My one thought was I couldn't let myself fall down. I just didn't know if I could get up again if I fell down. I read in the paper the next day that I had cut a corner and was disqualified. But I don't remember any of that."

Nienaber was disqualified in last Saturday's state run. Lloyd still won the race. Which indicates what kind of depth coach Mike Daley's Juggernauts had. Nienaber, you see, was the team's No. 4 man. Five count in cross-country scoring.

"I was in such pain after the race that I didn't realize we had won," Nienaber said. "I felt as if I had let everyone down. I was lying on the ground because I was too weak to get up. A photographer wanted to take a team picture, so everyone had to come over by me and some guys held me up.

"I knew we had won the race when I saw the guys with T-shirts on that said 'Erlanger Lloyd 1974 State Champs.' Coach Daley's wife had made those for us."

Nienaber, a senior, thinks Jerry Baynum, a freshman, deserves a lot of credit for Lloyd's big victory minus a man.

"Good old Jerry really came through," Nienaber said. " Cross-country is one sport where the fourth and fifth men are keys to the team score. The team actually depends on them to finish pretty high up. I wanted to do that Saturday, but I couldn't. I actually was surprised I was able to finish the race the way I felt."

Baynum placed 33rd for Lloyd. Sophomore John Adkisson came in 30th. They were the last two Lloyd runners to figure in the scoring behind Jude Baynum (second), Steve Adkisson (third) and Matt Huff (sixth).

When Nienaber was dizzy and half-conscious from his ordeal at the state meet, he was still able to make out some-

thing his coach said. It'll probably remain in his memory forever.

It was after the race and coach Daley was helping carry Nienaber back to the station wagon. Tates Creek's coach, whose team placed second behind Lloyd, asked Daley how his runners had done it. How had they won with their No. 4 man in such pain?

"Coach Daley told him it was kids like me who had made Lloyd the state champion," Nienaber said.

While he didn't take part in his team's winning score, Steve Nienaber was an integral part of the spirit which made Lloyd a state champion.

1974 Team Picture.
Spectator Yearbook photo.

STEVE ADKISSON

*"To have courage for whatever comes in life –
everything lies in that."*

-Mother Teresa (1910-1997)
Nobel Peace Prize winning missionary

After taking the week after the State Championship off from running, we jumped right back into a normal routine of training. Several of us competed in the AAU Cross-Country Championship race which was 5 miles. I finished 24th in 30:26 and during the next few weeks was sick with a bad cold. I managed a decent month of training in preparation for the spring track season and was running five to seven miles each day during this "off season."

December started out well.

*December 1 1 ½ miles of hard running in 6" snow, then
    2 easy*
December 2 Warmup 3 x 1mile very hard in snow
December 3 6 miles continuous at 6:00 pace (felt good)
December 4 6 miles easy
December 5 9 miles easy distance
*December 6 1 mile warmup; 10x110 strides 1 mile
    warmdown*
December 7 rest
*December 8 3 miles medium and 12 miles hiking in
    woods*
December 9 5 miles easy
*December 10 4 miles fartlek – I hurt my leg somehow,
    coach said it might be a pulled hamstring?*
*December 11-31 zilch hamstring torn, went to Dr. treat
    with whirlpool, heating pad, Bengay*

I had been lucky enough over two and a half years to have avoided any major injury. This hamstring injury was one of those things that didn't have an exact cause, which the Dr. referred to as a "trauma." I was running along in the cold weather and it started to ache but I was able to finish the run. It was only after I stopped that the pain became severe and over the next several days became worse. At first, I thought it would be like any other nagging injury I'd had, which in a young healthy body heals up quickly. As the days, and then weeks began to roll along and it didn't seem to be getting better I started fretting over the conditioning that was being lost by my inability to train. My teammates were going out after school every day to run and I would go to the locker room and spend twenty or thirty minutes in the whirlpool with very little noticeable relief.

The hamstring is among the strongest and largest muscles in the body and its contraction is what pulls the body forward while running. It becomes extremely strong from training for long distances, but at the same time it becomes tighter and less flexible as it is strengthened. I had been training virtually every day for over two years and had developed most of my habits and friendships around this daily act of running. It was a drastic change for me to sit around and do nothing.

I only went to my family doctor once to have it diagnosed and he recommended that I not run on it until it didn't hurt anymore. While this sounded sensible at the time, it was torture to me to wake up every day and know from the pain of just getting out of bed that today was not the day I would be trying to go back out for a run.

The days became weeks, and the weeks became months, and after a while I began to wonder if it was ever going to heal.

IV
SENIOR

"The truth is this: the march of providence is so slow and our desires so impatient; the work of progress is so immense and our means of aiding it is so feeble; the life of humanity is so long and that of the individual so brief that we often see only the ebb of the advancing wave and are discouraged. It is history that teaches us to hope."

-General Robert E. Lee
1870 (4 and ½ years after Appomattox)

The year 1975 began with me pouting around trying to "make" my leg better. I went to the pool with the swim team a few nights a week to try to get in some kind of workout, but kicking in the pool only made my leg sore again the next day. I became hypersensitive to every little twinge and ache, so I started doing everything I could to avoid reinjuring it. At first I figured that each day it would get a little better and so every week or so I would test it by jogging across a parking lot. Each time I would quickly know that it wasn't quite right and so I would continue to get in the whirlpool, sleep with a heating pad on it, and stretch it every day. A few weeks would go by and I would try again. Same result, week after week.

177

Little by little it improved, but never quite like I wanted it to and it was always noticeable. That is one of the worst things about a major injury: it becomes a constant reminder that you can't do the one thing that you would most like to do, which for me was going out to run. The hardest part was that I had been so fortunate to not get injured or sick for such a long period of time that I had developed a reputation among my friends as being the most resilient and dedicated runner on the team. It was as confusing to them as it was to me that this injury I had could keep me inside. A hamstring injury doesn't require a cast, or surgery which leaves scars to heal; it doesn't have any swelling or give any visual evidence that there is something wrong. The only way I even knew it wasn't healed was by feeling the pain when I tried to use it, and after a while I started to question whether it was phantom pain or real pain.

After three months of this rest, test, rehab, test, I finally decided it was as good it was likely to get, so on February 22 I went for an easy one mile jog on the track. My logbook over the next few weeks details these easy runs, the amount of time I spent stretching, and even the amount of time I spent in the whirlpool. Somehow I must have determined there was some measurable way to decrease pain the way you can increase fitness by spending more time training.

After a month of easy two mile runs, it became obvious to both me and Coach Daley that the hamstring was not improving and that no matter what I did, I was not going to be ready to run any track races at the level that I would have been satisfied with. The last entry for the track season was for April 9 when I wrote The End and blacked out with a thick pencil whatever it was I wrote on the bottom half of the page.

Over the next few months I went to the track meets to

watch my friends race, but I became diffident in the way I went about things. I managed to get my school work done, and I was able to work more for money with all the extra time I had by not running, but I was miserable.

On Saturday May 31st I woke up, dressed and went downstairs to the kitchen. The morning newspaper was laid out on the counter and I picked it up and took it into the living room. Our team had competed in the Regional Track Meet the night before and even though I was there and saw what happened, I always liked to see what the papers had to say about the events.

On the front of the sport's page, the news jumped out at me like a punch in the stomach: "American Distance Star Steve Prefontaine Dies In Auto Accident." As I read the headline and the brief description of the facts that were known, I had the sinking feeling of losing a close friend.

Eugene, OR. While returning from a party and after dropping off friend and distance champion Frank Shorter, Steve Prefontaine was driving down a familiar road, Skyline Boulevard, near Hendricks Park, when his car, a gold 1973 MGB, swerved left and hit a rock wall along the side of the street. The overturned car trapped Prefontaine underneath it. The first witness on the scene, who lived nearby, heard two cars, and then a crash. When he ran outside he was almost run over by the second car. He found Prefontaine flat on his back, still alive but pinned beneath the wreck. After attempting to lift the vehicle, the witness ran to get help. By the time he returned with others, the weight of the car had crushed Prefontaine's chest, killing him. He was 24 years old. The cause of the accident has not yet been determined.

Something about learning of the death of one of our

179

running idols left me with a sense of bewilderment. It took a long time for me to read this short passage, but I read it several times before setting the paper aside and going back up to my room. I took off my work clothes and dressed in running gear and headed back down the stairs.

"I'm going for a run," I told my mom and since I had not run in several months, it must have caught her off guard to see me head out the door as I had done thousands of times before.

I ran down the hill of my street and up to one of our favorite loops through the cemetery at Forest Lawn. I was completely unaware of any pain in my leg. I was just running. At the cemetery is a Children's Graveyard which had a sunken pool with a fountain in it. This was a favorite place to go and meditate and often the team would run to this place and hang out in the middle of our easy Friday run before a big meet.

I sat down near the small shallow pool. I had stopped feeling angry about what had happened to Pre and was just numb with the sadness of his tragic death.

Eventually, I snapped out of the fog I was in and ran home. I will never really know for sure if it was a final healing of my injury or an awakening caused by the shock of Pre's death, but I remember this day as the day I began taking myself seriously as a runner again. This revelation, that we only have so much time and we better make the most of it, was something that struck a large part of the running community across the world. Over the next ten years, the generation of American distance runners inspired by the life of Pre would be among the best ever in sheer numbers. Road racing, cross country, and track would see growth as never before in terms of not only participation but also in the high level of performance on every level from high school to international competitions.

JUGGERNAUTS

"I am only one, but still I am one. I can not do everything, but I can do something. I will not refuse to do the something I can do."

Helen Keller

June 14 (I think) – Today for some strange unknown reason I jogged 3 ½ miles with Jude, Denny, & Mark R. I felt ok

June 15 3 miles easy running with Mark Rhodes. My H.S. doesn't hurt. I don't even believe it.

June 16 Ran 3 miles with Robin on track. Felt ok

June 17 AM bike ride 6 miles, swam 35 lengths. Ran 3 with Jude in the cemetery. Found out about Jr. Olympic 1 mile walk. Did some race walking intervals 1x440, 1 x 220, 1x mile in 11:48 in 4 inches of water on track.

June 18 Ran 3 miles

During my 7 month purgatory of being a spectator, I've learned several things about running and myself (in general) 1) Running is a very natural, organic, wholesome activity. There shouldn't even be races. Competition takes the fun out of it. 2) I'm not gonna be so serious and/or worried about placing well or killing myself to get my times down. I'm just gonna enjoy running in itself and if I do well then that's ok too.

I must have believed this (at least at the time I wrote it) but I had too much of a competitive spirit to not compete. Somewhere along the way I read that race walking was easier on the hamstrings than actual running but it also was a good way to build aerobic endurance. I had never competed in any race where the objective was not to get from the start to the finish line as quickly as possible, so the added challenge of specific rules about having both feet in contact with the ground was very contrary to everything I had ever trained my body to do.

I caught on quickly and even though I knew it was not the same as running, I could feel my endurance returning as I did race walking intervals. It takes considerably more concentration to walk as fast as possible under the strict rules than it did for me to simply run. The tradeoff in terms of it taking longer to go one mile walking than one mile running was that I had to learn to keep my focus for a longer period of time. This was one of the things I missed most during my seven month layoff: not being able to spend time every day requiring my mind to focus the actions of my body. It sounds funny to say it but there must be something hard-wired into a human being which requires him to make these kinds of mind-body connections on a regular basis.

Evolution has rewarded the human who could survive the day to day challenge of paying attention to his surroundings and responding by going outside his comfort zone to get what he needed. Whether that be the simple process of finding something to eat or the ability to chase down an animal, or to harvest the abundance the earth provides on a seasonal basis. The ones who were willing to push themselves when some of the others were content to lay around and wait for whatever happened next were the ones who survived.

Over the next few weeks I gradually returned to running regularly, but I still added the race walking as another form of training. For the previous five months I had done a daily routine of yoga exercises which included a long breathing and meditation practice. I can only guess that it was a combination of time healing the torn muscle tissue and the effects of this gentler stretching that I had gradually been able to apply to my whole body. Surprisingly, after only a few weeks of running I felt like I was progressing to a level close to where I had left off in December.

Running only sixteen days in the month of June, I accumulated fifty miles. Unlike previous summers, we began meeting as a team informally on Monday evenings at school after the 4ᵗʰ of July. At the first team practice, I ran five miles with my teammates and discovered there were now some new talented runners who were coming into their own. Jeff Ogden, a junior, and Jim Clayton, a sophomore, had been with the team for a couple of years but had competed on the Junior Varsity team. Denny Heidrich, another senior who like Jude had been a classmate or ours since Catholic elementary schools days, had run track for the first time the previous spring and been very impressive in the 880 and 440. He had been training with Jude, Gerry, and my brother John since early in the spring and was in extremely good shape. These three were ready replacements for the three who had graduated. All of them perfectly fit the mode and character of our team and fully embodied the never-say-die spirit that our team was known for. If anything, they added a whole new chemistry to the team with the enthusiasm that their "newness" to the sport brought with them.

On July 8ᵗʰ, I traveled to Louisville with my mother to stay with my cousin Mark and his family. My mom was taking the examination necessary to get into Nursing School. She planned to go to college in the fall for the first time.

My plan was to get in a few days of quality training and to compete at the AAU Track Meet in the 1 Mile Race Walk being held in Louisville. Mark was a year older than me and attended Jesse Stuart High School where the track and cross country coach was Don Webber. Webber had been a great middle distance runner at the University of Kentucky and had a quality high school program that had helped Mark run some very fast times.

Mark had been one of my running idols from the very first steps I took. Before my family moved to Erlanger, we lived just a few blocks away from one another and were together constantly from the time I was born. After we moved away and we both became interested in running, he became an unwitting mentor to me. We corresponded by mail and some of these letters contained not only great training advice but also some of the funniest and eccentric cartoons ever to pass through the U.S. postal system. We took turns trading schmack about who was the better runner, who had the prettiest girlfriend, and who would beat whom at the different distances when we finally got to race each other in college. His school was one of the largest in Jefferson County and Lloyd was in a different small school division, so our paths never crossed in any of the high school meets.

Whenever we met at family gatherings, we would run together and spend hours talking about the different training we did. This was very educational for both of us because we each had excellent coaches who had completely different backgrounds and training philosophies.

Mark was always on the cutting edge when it came to music, running shoes, and relationships with girls. This particular trip turned out to be a key turning point in my recovery from the hamstring injury. Over the next few days, we ran five miles every morning and went to the track for some easy intervals in the evening. After that, we went out and walked for hours in the neighborhoods around his house talking about the coming season and all that had gone on in the last track season. He was very excited to be going to Murray State University which had one of the best middle distance running programs in the country. He had met most of the Murray team on his recruiting trip there. Most of them were English and several had already broken 4:00 for the mile so he knew he was going to a place where he would have to improve dramatically to have a chance at competing.

Steve Adkisson & cousin Mark Rhodes after a long run.
Author collection. Photo by Cynthia Easely.

The effect of our discussions on me was to re-light the desire to see how good I could become. Before I went to Louisville, I had been going through the motions of training, cautious about reinjuring my leg. After running pain free for several days and spending this time with Mark, I felt rejuvenated and ready to get back to training for my senior season of cross-country. I knew that even though some colleges look at the third place finisher in the State Championship, they would most likely not offer any kind of scholarship to anyone who had not proven they could win the big races. Mark inspired me to want to win again.

On the last day I was in Louisville, we both competed in the AAU Meet. Mark ran a 1:56 880 and I competed in the 1 Mile Race walk finishing 5th in 8:43. I was officially disqualified for not keeping contact with the ground at all times, but I was not in the least disappointed since I knew I was back to running again.

The very next day, my brother John and I went with the Ogden family to Fontana Village in North Carolina for a vacation on the lake there. Since there were five of our team members on this trip, we would begin every day with a long run on the trails before spending the day water skiing, playing tennis, or swimming in the lake. It was a great week of training for me and I could feel my fitness coming back. I was also amazed at how good John and Jeff had become in the time since I had been unable to run.

We were flying on the trails and did an eight mile run up to the Appalachian Trail where we passed a sign marking the top of the mountain at over 5,000 feet. I had left Jeff and John behind on the ascent and when they arrived at the top, we turned around and headed back down. For some reason, we all got somewhat carried away coming down the rocky trail and just as I was about to suggest we slow it down a little bit, John lost his footing and tumbled a pretty respectable distance down the side of the mountain. When we ran down to him he was sitting up with blood running out of several scrapes and cuts on face, legs, and arms. Seemingly unfazed, he jumped up and continued on down to the bottom where he submerged in a horse watering trough at the trailhead to clean the blood off.

The last week of July marked the end of our "preseason" training before we were scheduled to start regular daily team practice. It was among the best weeks of summer training I had ever completed:

JUGGERNAUTS

July 25 Butler Park – "Camp" 9 miles LSD 9

July 26 Butler Park – am warmup 1 mile 10 x 300 hard warmdown 1 mile p.m. – 1 hour continuous LSD total 11

July 27 2 miles at Butler nite: 8 miles LSD back I-275 at home total 10

July 28 am 3 miles, swim 1000 yards, 3 miles nite: warmup 2 miles, 3x880, 1x mile, 2 miles cooldown total 11

July 29 am 3miles, swim 1200 yards, 3 miles pm 5 miles hard at Summit Hills Total 11

July 30 8 miles fartlek at Valley Station with Mark (had fun) 8

July 31 am 6 miles pm 4 miles fartlek at Marydale total 10

STEVE ADKISSON

"Start by doing what is necessary, then do what is possible,
and suddenly you are doing the impossible."

-St Francis of Assisi (1182-1226)

It is common now for many high school cross-country teams to journey to a university or running organization's weeklong camp. While attending these camps, runners spend time concentrating their energy on developing the skills they'll need to compete successfully during the season. For many coaches, this week of dedicated training is a great way to begin the season, to get an idea of who has done the work during the early summer, and to get to know his athletes on a more personal basis. The agenda for many of these camps consist of twice daily running sessions, educational and motivational discussions by the camp sponsors or guest speakers, and recreational activities geared toward promoting team spirit and camaraderie among the young athletes.

Cross-Country Camp had a whole different meaning for the Juggernauts of the mid 1970's. Before there was such a thing as formal camps, our coach developed a similar concept of the weekend camp and implemented it on us. I'm sure that the final outcome was similar to the intentions outlined above, but there were a few bugs to work out in the program before it would ever develop into anything like they have today.

One of the first procedural modifications from the way coach did our cross-country camp would be to make everybody commute together. Our school didn't make the buses available to us, which meant that anybody who had a car got to drive a carload of runners to camp. A few of the guys on the team had cars, mostly hand-me-down early sixty cars that were sketchy at best. Most of them were the type of cars that you would only put a dollar or two's worth of gas in, since when it did finally quit for good you wouldn't want to have a full tank of gas invested in it.

Camp, in our case, was exactly that. Coach was an active member of the Army National Guard and had somehow wrangled the use of the National Guard Base at the entrance to General Butler State Park as our base of operations (OPSBASE) for a weekend. Carrolton, Kentucky is about an hour southwest from our school. A straight shot down a modern interstate highway. Only trouble was, interstate travel didn't interest us all that much.

Kentucky is a tangled web of rivers, two lane roads, and scenery that includes rolling hills covered with a variety of deciduous and evergreen trees. All of this is easily capable of detouring a carload of seventeen and eighteen year olds with a weekend away from home. We had met as a team at the school and divided into groups that consisted of two van loads of freshman and sophomores driven by somebody's moms, as many people who would fit in Jude's 69 Camaro, Coach's pickup with all the gear, and Herald's 67' Nova Super Sport with me, Johnny, J.C., and Gerry.

Coach and the moms had a simple plan of driving straight down the interstate, exiting at the exit nearest the National Guard Base and arriving at camp in about an hour. Jude and I had come up with an alternate route that looked closer as the crow flies but necessitated several stops along the way, the first of which was for cigars and a carton of Pepsi.

The second and more important stop was at a place that has since become legendary for the mudball fight that took place on that July afternoon in 1975. Sugar Creek crosses U.S. 42 and joins the Ohio River about 10 miles from Warsaw, Kentucky. A dirt and gravel road goes off 42 and about a quarter mile back the road is a place to park your car. Someone who hadn't heard about litigation had tied a hundred feet of rope to the top of a tree that hangs out over the creek which, this close to the Ohio River, is several hundred yards across. Directly below the tree, which sits twenty or thirty feet above the creek, is the deepest part of the channel. When you swing out and jump, you really have to try hard to go deep enough to touch the bottom. I know this to be true because we made several hundred attempts to touch the bottom.

After attempting to sound the channel one at a time without scoring, we developed a primitive point system based on time spent under water, the size of the splash made and the apparent pain endured upon entry. A clear winner was never determined because the contest was interrupted when Gerry discovered quite by accident that if you went another forty or fifty yards out in the water you could stand up. His accident happened in what we all believed was a suicide attempt as he swam away from shore in his confusion and disgust with the last dive he had made.

When he was about halfway across and we were preparing to send someone out to save him, Gerry stopped swimming and stood up with nothing but his feet and ankles under water. Eight soaked and sunburned runners, clad in cut-off blue jeans suddenly got religion.

You often don't recognize an epiphany when it is slapping you in the face, but in this case, everybody wanted a chance to walk on the water. In a matter of seconds the channel foamed with the diverse strokes of the untrained, high muscle mass, low buoyancy runners' attempts at swimming as fast as possible.

Which turned out to be pretty fast because two or three of us swam face first into the mud and sand bar that Gerry was standing on. Only trouble was we had not swum fast enough. Gerry had discovered a motherload of grimy packable sludge and had been bombing us good as we swam towards him. He had made only a few nonlethal hits, but by the time everyone was on the bar, the natural competitive juices had begun to boil and mudballs filled the air like martins after mosquitoes.

Somewhere along the way, a division of the bombardiers occurred. The two sides faced each other at about thirty paces and alternately ducked and stood up, packed and threw, attacked and retreated. As the fight continued, those who were born to be leaders led and those who were born to step behind their buddy stepped behind their buddy (usually immediately after hearing the announcement "INCOMING!"). Strategies evolved and the innate genius of the Baynum brothers, who as usual were on opposing armies, came up with the submarine warfare tactic. By holding your breath and diving into the deeper water, you could infiltrate enemy space and come up closer and unexpected for your launching mission. This hadn't gone on too long when the inevitable occurred.

Jude had loaded all tubes and disappeared into deep water along the starboard side of the bar. Several salvos of depth charges had missed their mark and visual contact had been lost. Now, Jude had a remarkable lung capacity, a high pain threshold, and a great left-handed throwing arm. As our side's most feared enemy, we were preparing for a last stand when he chose the time and place for his attack.

Gerry had many of his brother's natural gifts, but what he had the most of, and what he had going for him at this particular moment was the pure blind luck that has followed him most of his life. He fired off the luckiest launch of the day. And believe me, there had been some very lucky shots fired that had ended in direct hits.

Just at the moment when Jude burst through the surface

and set his feet in the sloppy sludge for a better throwing stance, his mouth opened wide in his attempt to breath in the minute's worth of air he'd just done without. As he gulped for air, the long graceful sloping parabola of Gerry's mudball ended at the roof of his mouth.

Many who witnessed this have never fully recovered. The faith we all put in the statistical unlikelihood of impossible events was shattered and thus a belief in the impossible was ignited. Jude though, didn't think it was very funny and he didn't even need to ask who threw it. When he finished coughing and gagging, and the rest of us finished laughing and gagging, he went straight for Gerry with the vengeance only a brother could have.

Fortunately for all concerned, he caught him on the shallowest point of the sandbar and the ensuing mud wrestling match would have been easy and safe to break up if it hadn't been so much fun to watch.

We finally arrived at camp some four hours late, but Coach was so glad to see us alive that he just told us to get changed and ready to stretch out. We took our stuff into the large barracks building that was really nothing more than a giant gymnasium. Each of us staked out some turf and rolled out our sleeping bags. We put on our running clothes and headed back outside where coach and all the younger runners were waiting for us under a huge sycamore tree.

"Now, fellas," Coach said. "We're gonna do an easy nine mile run to the back entrance of the park and back to here. I want the varsity runners to stay together and the j.v. runners to stay together. Don't go any faster than the slowest one in the group can go. Stay together."

We had all heard this concept explained on many occasions, and what it really meant to us was "Run the slowest guy into the ground." The trouble with this concept was that nobody on the varsity was really all that slow, and only half of us had just eaten three cheese coneys, a 16 oz. Pepsi, and two Snickers Bars. Swimming makes you hungry.

Coach was one of the most brilliant people working with teenagers I've ever known. He knew all the tricks likely to be undertaken, all about shortcuts ("There are no shortcuts to success") and could lay out a mean course. The nine-mile course in this case travels through "the rolling hills of central Kentucky" as they like to describe them in tourist literature. I've come to be a pretty good evaluator of hills and we in Kentucky gauge a hill by the Banana Test: if you drop a banana peel and it slides all the way to the bottom, you're on a hill. The hills at General Butler State Park have since become the site of the NCAA Mountain Bike Championship. Twenty years before that, coach had scoped them out as a pretty good place to train his cross-country team.

It was halfway up the big front hill that the cheese coneys started being tasted again. Being only about 90 degrees with 98% humidity, that rumbly feeling in the stomach started to get to us a little. Down the long hill to the back entrance, first one and then another runner went wobbling to the side of the road, into the woods, and either barfed or squatted in that nonsupport excellence only an experienced runner can maintain.

Coach had driven to the turnaround point with some water and one by one the runners started showing up. Coach was a little confused at first. He knew going in that many of us were in excellent shape and had worked hard to improve over the summer. When several of the j.v. runners came into view before some of his more experienced runners, he had that momentary glow that Shaquille O'Neal's seventh grade basketball coach must have experienced when his question was answered: "Yes, coach, I'm only twelve years old."

Reality turned up in the pale and green-around-the-gills faces Coach encountered when everybody finally made it to the turnaround. Funny thing about getting sick when you're running: you go from feeling like you would rather just have somebody start shoveling the dirt in to never better in the time it takes to say "Ralph." A cup of water and a minute of standing still later, we were back to as close to normal as most of us would ever be and off running up the back hill.

If you think about it, and be honest, there are really very few competitive runners who don't at some point in a group running situation want to just run off and leave everybody puffing in their dust. When you have seven or eight people whose fitness levels are similar, this can become a very painful experience for all concerned. When it happens on a daily basis, one of two things happens: extremely effective training or attrition. Some days you can't tell the two apart.

Somewhere near the top of the hill, the group silently decided to declare "Uncle" and when everybody had caught up - Jude, Johnny, J.C., Denny, Gerry, Herald, Jeff, and me - the long gentle downhill glide to the barn became what team running is really all about: that calm, graceful feeling of being part of a wild pack, a member of the great human herd.

JUGGERNAUTS

DAYBREAK

Again this procession of the speechless
Bringing me their words
The future woke me with its silence
I join the procession
An open doorway
Speaks for me
Again

-W.S. Merwin

Coach knew us well enough by now that he could tell by just glancing around at our faces how things were going. He knew how we had spent the summer and how his main job was being a set of reins rather than a bullwhip. He had never asked our adjuration of all the common vices and had never expressly demanded respect, but had earned it anyway. The experienced members of the team had gained their experience with him being aware of nearly every step we took between August and May

On the first day of practice he had us run an easy two miles to warm up and then gathered us under the big maple tree in front of the school and told us to sit down. This was unusual, first that we were having a meeting, and second that he thought it was going to last too long for us to have it standing up. I could sense a seriousness in Coach that we had not seen before.

"Now fellas, I've been thinking all summer about what this year was going to be like."

He paused for a minute going through his thoughts. I glanced sideways at Jude and he was looking up at Coach with the same furrowed brow that I must have been wearing.

"We have five seniors on the team this year, but we've lost three who ran in the State Meet last year. Those are going to be tough shoes to fill. As the defending State Champions, we are going to have a big bull's eye on our shirts all season. We are not going to surprise anybody anymore. Every time we run, the other teams are going to be gunning for us. We've never been in that position until now and I want to make sure everyone understands there is only one way for us to handle this kind of situation and that is to keep doing what we've been doing. We don't have enough talent on this team to take anything for granted. We will have to outwork all the other teams in the state to win another state championship, just like we did in the past. But before we even think about the State Championship, we have to outwork Highlands and Covington Catholic and Holmes and Dixie. I guarantee everyone here that those coaches and those teams have not stopped thinking about what happened to them last year and how you snuck up on them from out of nowhere. They have you in their sights and they are out to beat us. You can bet on it."

The thought which entered my head at that moment was "I wonder who is wearing their 'Kentucky State Champion' shirt." As proud as I was of owning one, along with a limited edition wind breaker with the school logo and "State Champ" across the back, and the belt buckle my dad had made of the medal the state awarded us, I had stopped wearing this gear when my injury forced me to give up running. I felt like I was starting all over again, that I had to prove everything all over again, and I think this was what Coach was really looking for the whole team to do.

I did a quick scan and saw that none of the four of us who had been on the team the previous year was flying the colors. Jude, Gerry, and John all had on one of their standard nasty running tee shirts. This was somehow reassuring to me and I gave my attention back to Coach as he finished his speech.

"This ain't gonna be no pushover fellas. We're gonna have to get back to pickin em up and putting em down like we've always done. We are nowhere near as deep a team as we were last year. Matt Huff, Steve Nienaber, and Dave Crump were consistently our 3, 4, and 6 runners. All 7 spots on the varsity and all 7 spots on the junior varsity are wide open. We'll do like we've always done it. The seven fastest runners will be the varsity and the next seven will be the junior varsity. This can change every week depending how you perform in the last race."

"When it comes time to enter people in the big meets, we are going with the best seven we have, no matter what grade you're in. Last year, Gerry Baynum, as a Freshman, won the team the State Championship when Steve Nienaber got sick. If I had decided that I would run all the seniors in the State Meet, we would have ended up second or third. Some schools run kids in Junior High, and if any of you 7th and 8th graders can be in the top seven, you will run in the Regional and State Meets."

"For you new fellas here, I'll go over the rules." Coach looked over at me and saw I was smiling. I watched a flicker of a laugh come to his face as he knew I was the only one who had heard all four of these "First Day" speeches. Coach and I had the kind of relationship in which most things "go without saying," but this was only because he knew me and where I came from, how I was raised. I respected his totalitarian system without question because it was the way it had always been since my first day of practice four years ago. The things he was about to say would be redundant to me, but as the man in charge of a team which had swelled to forty, he had to say them anyway – just to make it crystal clear.

197

"Number one, you're late if you're not ten minutes early. We start practice fifteen minutes after school lets out. Stretch out on your own and be ready to run when I get there. Most of you have met Mr. Hinsdale. He will be my assistant again this year and there are likely to be some times when I can't be here at all. He is the coach when I'm not here. If he tells you a rooster can pull a freight train, hook him up. Everybody got it?"

"Number two, when you can't be here, let somebody know."

"Number three, we're going to be traveling more this year and I want to make sure everyone understands we choose the traveling squad the same way. The school will only pay for fourteen students to go, but we will try to set up some car pools for anybody else who wants to come along to watch."

Coach looked over the paper he had on top of his clipboard, making sure he had covered everything. "Oh yeah. One more thing. We're going to have another camp at the end of the month. My guard unit ok'd us to come back down for the weekend of August 22. I know some of you who work couldn't get off for the last one, so I wanted to give you some notice if you want to go."

"The weekend after that, for those of you who think you can handle it, we will go to the Charleston, West Virginia fifteen miler. Fifteen miles is a long way, but I think some of you are ready for it."

Coach looked around the group again just to make sure there were not any questions.

"Ok, let's get going."

August 22 9 miles fartlek at Butler Park

August 23 5 mile road race at Butler Park 31:00 pm 40 min fartlek

August 24 am 1 hour hard fartlek 4x880 4x660 enroute

August 25 1 mile warmup 12 x 440 at 75-77 2 mile warmdown

August 26 am 5 miles pm 8x220 untimed but fast (for me) 1 mile warmdown

August 27 I felt rotten today with an ear infection – 1 mile easy

August 28 Woke up with sore hamstring. Stretched and jogged 2 miles   Meet – CCH, St Henry's at LHS 2ⁿᵈ 10:32, felt ok

August 29 Travel to Charleston, W.V. Stretched and ran 2 miles H.S. tight

August 30 Charleston 15 mile Road Race 418ᵗʰ 1:50:23. Felt ok. H.S. tight but had fun

August 31 Stretch, ran 5 miles very easy, felt ok

<u>*August Finals*</u> *267 Miles in 31 days for 8.5 miles per day avg. (not bad) Ran 1 2 mile race in 10:32 Also Raced 15 mile road race at Charleston*

The Charleston 15 Miler was one of the early elite road races which attracted many of the nation's outstanding distance runners. The 1975 edition paid a special tribute to Steve Prefontaine and all participants received a black sleeveless shirt with "A Salute To Pre" printed on the back. All of us who competed in the race proudly wore these shirts as often as possible to practice, and for the rest of the season there was not a day we ran when someone didn't have their Pre shirt on.

The Charleston race was as challenging a fifteen mile course as anyone could have invented. The first few miles were a long gradual hill up the river valley and while we were running we could hear the constant whop whop of helicopter blades as the media followed the leading men and women and filmed the race from above. As the leaders grew further and further ahead of the rest of us mid-pack runners, the helicopter sound faded into the distance.

After the long uphill the road course dropped back down to the river valley and the last nine or ten miles was along the river where the course was fairly easy, even though the heat was oppressive. None of us ran particularly well in the race, but every one of us finished in respectable times.

This finish takes place at Laidley Field, a local community college track, and as my brother John and I sat in the upper row of bleachers waiting for the rest of our team to finish, John was struggling to untie his wet and "triple knotted" training flats. An older gentleman was sitting nearby and John asked him if had a pocket knife he could borrow to cut his laces.

The man reached into his pocket and took out his knife and handed it to John while asking how we had done in the race. John answered that we'd done ok, that we were high school runners getting ready for our cross-country season.

The man told us he had gotten to fly around watching the race in the helicopter. John got the gleam in his eye that any kid who dreams of flying gets when someone mentions being airborne in any way possible. At age three, John had made himself a pair of cardboard wings and tried to fly off the top of the doghouse in our backyard.

He said, "Wow, that must have been something!"

"Yes," the man answered. "Steve would have liked a race like this. He would have been proud to know that so many people honored him in this way."

For a minute, John and I looked at each other like "What is he talking about?" "Steve?" we were thinking.

"Steve who?"

Suddenly it occurred who this might be. John said, "Are you Mr. Prefontaine?"

"Yes. They asked me to come to be the honorary starter and I was glad to come. I know how much this would mean for the running community who has done so much for us since the accident."

Neither of us really knew what to say, but when John handed his knife back to him he said, "Thank you so much." We shook his hand and he wandered away as several of our other teammates came up to where we were sitting and John told them what had just happened. By this time, several others in the crowd had recognized him and a line of autograph seekers was forming as runners and other fans formed a line to meet and the shake the hand of Ray Prefontaine.

CINCINNATI ENQUIRER September 2, 1975
Successful Running Means Hard Work,
And Erlanger Lloyd Best in Area

By Herb Whitney Kentucky Sports

Distance Runners have always intrigued me. They aren't noticed by many fans, they aren't accorded much space by newspapers, but still they go through the agony and the loneliness which is their daily domain.

As a sportswriter in Louisville for five years, I did something every fall which my colleagues found slightly amusing. I wrote about cross-country runners.

I think my fellow writers' smirky attitude reflects the way most people view high school runners. They ask: Are those kids some kind of nuts or something?

*Perhaps I can help here. Two characteristics I've no-
ticed about most good long-distance runners in high school
are: (1) They tend to be more intelligent than the average
student. (2) They are too small to excel at other sports, but
they have the desire to excel athletically.*

*Let there be no doubt about what kind of hard work
cross-country runners go through day after day, week after
week. This isn't a seasonal sport. It's year-round. The best
runners never stop running, so to speak.*

*Mike Daley brought that point home to me a few days
ago. I asked the Erlanger Lloyd High School coach how
many miles one of his boys would cover in four years, including meets and practices. His estimate was 20,000
miles.*

*That's equivalent to running back-and-forth across this
country a little over three times, or to put it another way:
almost enough to circumnavigate the planet.*

*"It sounds like an awful lot, but it doesn't take real long
to cover that kind of distance," Daley said. "That 20,000
figure includes track meets and practices, too. Most cross-
country runners also run the mile or two-mile in track."*

*Daley says he's never seen a fat distance runner. "A
boy usually has to be slim to keep going," he said. "And
the longer the distance, the smaller the runner is.*

*"There are qualities that all good runners display in-
stinctively. A forward lean, arms below chest level, a kind
of glide in their movement. Some kids come out and run like
that from the start and you know you've got something
when they do."*

*Daley is entering his fourth season as cross-country
coach at Lloyd which posted a school-best 10-2 won-lost
record his first year at the helm. Two years ago, Lloyd finished fourth in the state Class AA meet after capturing both
the Ninth Region and Northern Kentucky Athletic Confer-*

ence championships. Last year, they won the Class AA State Championships after dominating northern Kentucky's Conference and Regional meets.

"We don't just practice distance running," Daley pointed out. "We'll also have the kids do interval sprints – some 440s and 880s. A good runner needs to run a long way, but he also must be able to sprint at the end."

When Daley came to Lloyd, the squad numbered about 10. That's up to 35 now.

"They were mostly real young kids when I first got here," he said. "Now we've got those same ones and a lot of younger ones, too. But the thing with cross-country is it takes time to become competitive. A runner usually can't help the varsity much until he's a sophomore. A lot of practice time is spent logging miles, building them up for some future day."

Summer is a special time for Daley and his runners. "I'm in the National Guard, and I go to camp every summer down at General Butler State Park in Carrolton," Daley said. "I take my runners and we stay in the armory. We get to run a lot and it doesn't cost anything except for meals."

The rest of the year, Lloyd's runners do their sprints at the high school and distance work at such places as Devou Park and Summit Hills Country club.

"It's a year-round sport," Daley said. "Sometimes I have to explain why it's this way to parents, and how running will be beneficial to their sons. Their sons spend a lot of time working hard for me and the parents want to know why.

Daley can see the growth of his favorite sport in terms of increased attendance at meets.

"My first year at Lloyd we'd draw 15 or 20 people to a dual meet," he said. "Now the school seems to be caught

*up in winning and we draw around 100. Our fans have vi-
sions of going to the state again and winning it. I think we
have a good chance, too."*

The added fan participation pleases Daley.

*"Cross-country runners are athletes and they want to
be recognized as athletes," he said. "Frank Shorter's winning the marathon in the 1972 Olympics brought more attention to distance running in this country. Any kind of
publicity really helps the kids."*

Well, here's some more.

Even with all the recognition our team was getting, and
as well as our summer of training had prepared us for an
amazing senior season, the year was off to a chaotic start.
As important as running was to us, there were many world
changing events that put our small town dreams of repeating as State Champions into perspective. Saigon had fallen
and the war in Vietnam was rattling to a halt. The draft was
being abolished so those of us who would turn eighteen
over the next year could at least have a choice about mili-
tary service. On September 5th, there was an assassination
attempt on President Ford made by a crazed Squeaky
Fromme, one of the Manson family of psychopaths hell-
bent on creating Helter Skelter on the world.

Nearly everyone on the team was a fan of the Cincinnati Reds and they were winding up an amazing year in
which they would win 108 games, going 64 – 17 at Riverfront Stadium. Many of us had attended as many home
games as we could get free or cheap tickets to, and the
whole region was buzzing with World Series hopes for the
Big Red Machine.

Despite the seemingly daily distractions, our September
training included a lot of miles and a return to many of our
basic interval workouts. Jude was in phenomenal shape and

even though I had come back as strong physically as I had ever been, he had the edge in his confidence. I raced him hard every time out, but he was just mentally stronger.

I finished second to Jude in the Covington Catholic Invitational where my big breakthrough race had come the year before. Our team scored only thirty-one points as our three through seven runners had made the same kind of improvements Jude and I had made and it was making a big difference in the confidence they had in themselves to race hard against any and all competition.

We continued to race twice and sometimes three times a week, but it was not unusual for several of us to do another tempo run or interval workout after one of the dual meets. I was determined to improve my finishing speed and so I would often go over to the track after a cross-country race and do an interval session of 4 x 440 below 70. I believed running fast when I was already fatigued from a race was the best way to push myself to the next level of fitness I was going to need to catch back up with Jude.

Coach Daley's National Guard Unit was called up and deployed early in the month to help the Louisville police control race riots brought on by the school system's implementation of a new busing plan. For a week, Louisville was the scene of bitter and violent civic strife because of court-ordered busing designed to integrate the local schools. White parents, whose kids were forcibly bussed to traditionally black schools, protested by pelting the buses with rocks and eggs. The police and National Guard in helmets and riot gear worked around the clock to protect the buses and school children from the demonstrators. The Ku Klux Klan was found to be the chief rabble rouser and outside agitator in what was essentially a resistance to change on the part of the parents. Eventually, the protests died down as tensions eased and the idea of racially integrated schools became accepted by both whites and blacks. Louisville school officials made adjustments to their plan that gave parents much more choice in where their children attended schools.

The team followed the events by reading the newspaper accounts of what was going on in Louisville, and there were a few days where we worried about Coach's safety but when he came back he told us he was never in any real danger. He mostly rode in a patrol car with a suburban police officer to be a backup. "Just in case," he said.

During the time Coach Daley was gone Coach Hinsdale took over as head coach and directed our daily workouts. We went about our training and racing without much disruption even though it was certainly a little different in terms of control over the activities of the team. Coach Daley could put the fear of God in you. Coach Hinsdale was such a fun-loving, easy going guy that some of us older runners had a hard time taking him seriously. It wasn't any kind of disrespect for his authority, but it probably had something to do with all the other interactions we had with him outside of school. When he hired us out to work for him at his farm, he was more of a friend than a boss. He knew us and appreciated us for who were without necessarily needing to be the totalitarian leader Coach Daley was. When he sent us out for a long road run, he knew we would do at least as many miles as he had instructed. Coach Hinsdale would often run with the J.V. runners and let the varsity go out on our own.

One of our new favorite places to run was "The Valley" which was a large tract of land owned by various developers. The land was too hilly and steep to be used for housing developments. In fact the only real activity going on over the thousand acres was the riding of motorcycles and the mudslinging of four wheel drive vehicles. The trails developed by the ongoing dirt bike traffic were a perfect place for us to do our longer runs. Over the course of several weeks we had explored The Valley enough to know where all the steep hills were and we would run a long loop which included several of these hills, getting in ten to twelve miles in our after school runs. It was not unusual to see deer, turkeys, and even a pack of wild ponies that we would chase up and down the hills. We came close on several occasions but were never able to actually catch one. The Baynums had vowed to ride one of the ponies back into town if we ever actually got hold of one, but since no one ever carried ropes or other horse tackle, I doubt if it could have been pulled off – though that didn't stop us from trying.

Just before Coach Daley finished his Guard Duty in Louisville, several of us had gotten comfortable enough with Coach Hinsdale's loose reins that we went considerably across the lines of expected behavior. We were getting perilously close to out-of-control when we finally had to have a reality check.

STEVE ADKISSON

"So strange had been the apparition of these men, their dress had been so allied in colour to the soil, their passing had so little disturbed the solemn rumination of the forest, and their going had been so like a spectral dissolution, that a witness could have wondered if he dreamed."

-Stephen Crane

Most high schools have underground histories or local legends that have evolved over decades with the phenomenon of the whisper chain: A tale is whispered to one who whispers it to another who says "Huh? . . . Oh yeah" and then whispers a completely different version next week to another who half hears it and then retells it to another. The result is that a true story gets both embellished and diminished by time and the absence of truthful detail.

After consulting with my attorney, who tells me that most likely the statute of limitations has expired on the crimes involved in this tale, I have decided to clear up the mystery of the disappearing Juggernaut Ziggurat.

For those of you who don't know what a Juggernaut is, I would suggest the definition displayed on the tee shirts of our football team: "A massive inexorable force, campaign, movement, or object that crushes whatever is in its path," or "From the Hindi word *JagannaAth,* literally, lord of the world, the common title of Vishnu." Think of it as a gladiator on steroids, or as we commonly said a "Trojan XL."

A ziggurat, on the other hand, is simply a temple tower of the ancient Assyrians and Babylonians, having the form of a terraced pyramid of successively receding stories [from the Akkadian zaqaru, to build high].

I learned this in my first period "Free Reading" class where our teacher had just a few rules in the class. The first rule was that as long as we were reading or appeared from the outside to be reading we could go at our own pace and be left alone. The second rule was that if you stumbled on a word whose meaning you did not know, you had to look it up in the dictionary. The teacher had privately established a separate rule for me that I had to study every word on the dictionary page of the word I looked up.

The word ziggurat was one of the half dozen words on the page that had a picture beside it and when I saw the picture, it got my attention. A few nights before, five of us had been on a night run which was usually a four mile round trip from our house up to the school and back. We jumped the fence and entered the football field, and with the innocent intention of exploring the infrastructure beyond the "No Students Allowed" sign, scampered up the grandstand and climbed on top of the press box just to see what we could see from up there.

The football field press box has a ladder to the roof where the football coaches can watch the game from a birds-eye view, radio down their suggestions for improving the team's performance, and keep an eye on the student body. Being one of the student body who needed an eye kept on him, I had felt the hot eyes of a particular football coach on many Friday nights.

Coach Dillon, for whatever reason, had something against me. Seemed like every time I looked up at him, he was looking down me. Or so I believed. As many a 17-year old is prone to do, I had what turned out to be delusions that the world conspired against me. But I didn't learn they were delusions until many years later, and it seemed to me at the time that he was going out of his way to get me in trouble.

Maybe I gave him some reason. The fact that he had caught me running at top speed down the hallway back to class (after I had just been sent to the office for eating my lunch during homeroom) didn't seem like much of a reason to me. I was late to a class I really needed to be paying attention in so I was in a hurry to return.

He sent me back to the principal's office where, in his surprise to see be back again so soon, the assistant principal asked me the same question he had asked me five minutes before: "You want three licks or two days detention?" I turned around and bent over again.

Our press box had an eight-foot tall chair bolted to the roof to give the coach who sat in it just that little bit more elevation that might make a difference in a game of inches. The chair was made of four-inch steel pipe welded together like a four-sided ladder. It had a padded back and arms. Standing guard over the football field, the tower of the home stands, press box, and chair had the same exact shape as the ziggurat in the dictionary picture.

"You guys know what we're standing on?" I said, anxious to spring my new word on them.

"Yeah. The press box," Gerry said.

Everybody looked at me in anticipation of some enlightening new name or concept. We were accustomed to sharing various embellishments of trivialities about the world we lived in. Some of them were truly innovative and some of them were just plain silly, so I looked around the faces and made a judgment call that nobody was ready for this one.

"Nevermind," I said and kept my ziggurat to myself.

"Mission tonight," I announced to my brother John, Jude, Beaves, and Denny when we finished showering after cross-country practice. They were all surprised to hear me make any kind of announcement as I hardly ever said anything, let alone in the day or two after getting "licks" from the school disciplinary personnel. What had brought it up was when Jude had remarked on my "rough day," having heard from his girlfriend, who was the office aid when I had made my second trip to the principal's office, about what had occurred that day.

After supper and chores and some homework, John and I dressed to go out for our normal night run. We went by Denny's and headed up toward the Baynum house where Jude and Gerry were waiting out on their porch when we got there. From anyone watching, it would have looked like any five teenagers out for an easy run as we crossed the highway. It was not unusual to see us running any time from seven to midnight depending on the season. In early September, it was full dark by 8:30 and we ran to the school by the same route we always used.

Once on the school grounds we slowed to a walk and checked out the surroundings. Seeing it all clear, we dropped out of the light into the woods that circled the back half of the football field. We climbed the fence and walked across the blackness of the football field. We climbed the press box like we had done a few nights earlier, but once we were up there, I revealed my plan to them by taking a socket wrench out of my sleeve and unwrapping the thirty feet of rope from around my waist.

I had originally thought about simply loosening the bolts on the chair and waiting for Friday night, but I already had a thorough grasp of the concept of karma and I didn't think that the coach had built enough good karma to pass on to a better next life. The plan B was to simply remove his chair and wait for Friday night and watch from a distance as he and rest of the coaching staff puzzled over their discovery right as the game started.

It was a pretty good plan too except that the chair weighed about 300 pounds and the rope I brought must been something like 80 lb. test. We laid down on our stomachs while my plan manifested itself to the others. Gerry giggled. Jude poked his head up and looked all around, seeming a little bit anxious.

"How did you know what size socket to bring?" Johnny asked me.

"Lucky guess, the first time I brought it up." I said. Pausing for the effect I knew it would have on them, I added "I was up here last night too."

This got their attention a little bit.

"Nuh unh," Jude said. "Secret miles?"

"I thought I smelled Kroil", Johnny said, referring to the rust break I had sprayed on the bolts in my scouting mission.

"Like I said."

I loosened the bolts and gathered them together. Plan B was becoming pretty obvious to everyone even though I hadn't really spelled it out. Johnny got up on his knees and gave a long look all around.

"Hold on," he said.

At the far end of the parking lot, headlights were shining on the couple of cars left overnight at the school. We lay there quietly waiting to see what the car would do. It came on through the parking lot and passed under the five sets of eyes peering out from under the railing.

When the car was completely out of sight, we scooted the chair to the back edge of the press box and tied the rope to it. Two of us held the rope while the others tried to quietly ease the chair up and over the railing. Once balanced on the railing, the two of us holding the rope got a good grip, and nodded ok to the others who pushed it out.

About the same time that the chair seesawed to the heavy-end-down position, the rope was already maxed out, and the chair balanced precipitously on the handrail and continued its descent with barely a pause to test the rope. It banged on the side of the press box, and then crashed on down in an impressive tectonic display on to the mostly gravel landing pad.

All five of us had already "hit the deck" as soon as we saw what was about to happen, and we lay frozen in fear as the silence rushed in to fill the vacuum left when the crash was over. After a minute or so had passed without hearing any sound of alarm, we slipped one by one down the ladder and tip-toed down the aluminum bleachers. We circled around to where the chair had landed. Beaves, who was never without words, said "Where we gonna put it, Hadley?"

I thought for a minute, and then said "I don't know but let's try to get it to the fence." The five of us could carry it, just not very fast. In our haste to move it, we stumbled and cussed about how heavy it was. We managed to get it to the fence. There was a thick woods on the other side of the fence that we didn't know much about, but I figured if we just got it out of site, they would probably be a long time finding it. We struggled to lift it up, balanced it on top of the barbed wire, and heaved it over. It fell with a thud into the soft ground and we all followed over and drug it about twenty feet into the woods before we stopped to rest a minute and pull briars out of our arms and legs, figuring out what to do next.

Having lost track of time, I was surprised when I looked at my watch and discovered that it had only been about fifteen minutes since we had hopped over the fence and started climbing the ziggurat. It seemed an eternity and I knew we couldn't risk being around the school grounds much longer.

"Let's just get it into the woods a little further and figure out what to do with it later," I suggested.

There was no disagreement, but I don't think I was the only one who had that sinking feeling in my stomach that this was probably not the last time the subject of this chair would come up.

It only took about twelve hours to find out. After the principal had tapped the microphone to the intercom signaling morning announcements the very next day, he began his comments: "If the students who took the chair from the press box will come forward and return the chair today, the school system will not press criminal charges. If the chair is not returned today, the police will be notified and it will no longer be a school matter . . ."

Now, we all know there is a very real difference between a prank and a crime. There may be some gray area in this matter, but I wasn't going to be the one debating it with either the principal or the local law enforcement officers. I had a hard time getting the phrase "thicker than thieves" out of my mind that day, but we had not had any discussion about the advisability of having a story to stick to when we ran home from school the night before.

I trusted the Baynum brothers and Denny completely. John was my flesh and blood brother and I knew he wouldn't say anything, but I kept wondering if anybody had let it slip to somebody else they trusted. The fewer people who knew about it, the better, but when you are seventeen, sometimes people say things to impress people when they should, and in fact even do, know better.

All day long, students were asking each other if anybody knew anything about what the principal was talking about. It was really big news in a school with just 800 students. The more people talked, the more puzzling it became because surely somebody at the school knew something about what had happened. Nothing. Nobody claimed even false responsibility for the chair's disappearance, which was a little surprising because there were some truly bad kids who would normally have taken credit for something that would have raised their rep amongst their peers.

Some even asked "What chair?" in their ignorance about the existence of the press box chair.

As the day wore on, the subject of the chair continued to dominate the between-class discussions. I kept having that same gnawing feeling in my stomach, but I managed to plead ignorance when the subject came up, even to the point of changing the subject.

"You know what workout Coach has us doing today?" I asked one of my teammates who wasn't with us the night before.

He didn't know, but I answered for him with "I guess we'll find out," as he walked away looking over his shoulder at me like "what's wrong with you?"

It is uncanny how sometimes when you deserve punishment, you very often get it even if you can't exactly associate the specific act you are being punished for with the specific punishment you are receiving. This seemed to happen a lot when it came to our team and the training that Coach had prepared for us. Maybe it wasn't always planned, but near the end I had a suspicion that Coach was omnipotent – that or he had one of those crystal balls that allowed him to monitor every move we made and adjust the workout accordingly.

Coach Daley had just arrived back after his Guard Duty in Louisville and this was to be his first day of practice with us. Whatever the reason, the workout we did that day put a real hurtin on all of us and when we were finished, coach had us sit down for a rare "sit down" meeting. Coach was not one to go on and on about anything. He said something once and that was it. Meeting over.

But this day's meeting was two days before the biggest

invitational meet so far this season and would be a real test of how well we had replaced the graduating seniors and maybe he just wanted to remind us about a few things. I knew something wasn't exactly right when coach came walking up to the group with a socket in his hand. I swallowed hard and felt the boom boom of my heart getting a big dose of adrenaline. There were forty of us standing there, and five of us with weak knees and extremely serious expressions on our faces.

His message to us that day went along these lines: "Now fellas, this meet isn't gonna be no pushover. All the schools we can expect at State are gonna be there and they are gunning for us. Franklin County is tough and so is Owensboro. After this workout today, I don't want you putting in any extra miles. I don't want to hear about any of you 'cootin around' at night. That goes for everybody," he said as his eyes met mine and he made sure to look up and down the line of us older runners.

The whole time he was talking, he was spinning the socket around in his hand.

We all nodded agreement and kept eye contact, each afraid of giving away the slightest hint of guilt that was spilling over the top in at least five of us.

The next day at morning announcements, the principal let it be known they had turned over their evidence to the police and that fingerprints had been taken at the scene of the crime. The prints were clear and the police were certain they would be able to identify the thieves if they did not surrender voluntarily.

I pretended to be reading. I came upon a word I didn't know. "Usurp" was another word on that dictionary page. I decided to consider that we had simply usurped the ziggurat for unspecified (at this time) future purposes.

No one from the school administration ever found the

lost chair, although I bet it hasn't moved an inch since we deserted it the woods not fifty feet from the fence. I've glanced over that way a few hundred times over the rest of that year and seen that the woods have grown thick with briars in that general area. We talked about relocating the chair on several occasions, but never could come up with an idea good enough to justify the possible expulsion, loss of eligibility, or time in the big house that getting caught would have meant.

They most likely did have fingerprints, but the nanotechnology required to quickly match prints was still years away and mine have never been entered into the database anyway.

I've probably been punished enough.

STEVE ADKISSON

Go Ask Alice
Upon First Observation

-The Tatler, Volume I 1975

Here we go again. I sat under the maple tree the first day of cross-country practice and sketched the blurs of the passing runners as they winnowed by the tree. Blur number one, hair streaming out behind what I can only describe as a gliding quasar of infinite energy, has a name: Jude Baynum. You may have seen him too, if you looked fast enough.

Blur number two, described last year in the Kentucky Compost as being "no bigger than a minute" also has a name, and a heart that would exceed the measuring capacity of the Grinch's branding iron at ten sizes too big: Steve Adkisson.

The two Lloyd seniors led the Juggs to their first State Championship last year, and seem primed to inculcate what should have been already learned by their competitors.

Blur number one was slowed by a virus in that meet but rebounded to set track records in the spring. Blur number two missed all of the track season with a torn hamstring suffered last winter. Despite these setbacks, which both consider ancient history, I can tell you there is a zip in their step, and a do-dah in their auras, that I have never before witnessed in my close up inspections over their entire high school careers.

It looks like the Juggs are set to resume their hegemony over the cross-country teams in not only the region but the Commonwealth as well.

In their first meet of the season held Tuesday against

JUGGERNAUTS

Dixie Heights, the entire Juggernaut team subjugated the visiting Colonels, scoring a perfect 15 points. For those of you unfamiliar with cross-country scoring this means Lloyd's runners placed 1, 2, 3, 4, &5 – before the first opponent came across the line. In the common lexicon it means Lloyd kicked their #*(.

If you are reading this and you plan to race against Blur one and Blur two this year, I have a three word incontrovertible recommendation for you: 'pack a lunch' – it's gonna take all day.

Like any seventeen year-old senior in high school, I had a need for cash. In the pecuniary society we lived in, it was possible to have fun without money but having enough for even small extravagances was an ongoing challenge for everybody I hung out with. My folks worked as hard as possible to provide all nine of us with a place to live, enough to eat, clothes to wear, as well as some extras. But it was tough to expect them to be able to give us spending money too. I had worked as a paperboy for several years, a job that was handed down from my older brother to me, then to my two younger brothers as they were able to do it. It paid one penny per paper and there were 192 houses on the route. You had to hang the paper on the doorknob and deliver them four times a week. On Thursday, we delivered the Dixie News which was the local newspaper and on the other days, we delivered circulars advertising all the discounts for the local stores. I know doing this job for a few years must have developed some cardiovascular fitness because I would try to do it as fast as possible so I could get back out to play ball somewhere.

I worked summers and winters when I wasn't running cross country and track at the local Holiday Inn, and even had a summer job umpiring the local women's softball league as part of my job on the Erlanger Recreation Staff. If you ever need a lesson in sportsmanship, grab a facemask and get behind the plate as an umpire.

Several of my friends farmed and were regularly in need of additional hands for hay season, tobacco season, cattle and pig castration and vaccinating, and fence building projects. The Hensley family's farm was closest to my house, and since Herald ran on the team they were naturally my favorite family to work with. In my junior year, Jim Hinsdale came to teach English and volunteered as an assistant cross-country coach, a position made necessary because of the great recruiting job Coach Daley had done bringing the team numbers up to more than twenty-five runners. Coach Hinsdale wore a Fu Man Chu mustache and was also a runner, which allowed him to not only keep an eye on us out on the road, but also to be a great influence on the athletes he worked with. His friendly and generous nature made him a great addition to our team.

Coach Hinsdale and his father owned a couple of farms and when he found out some of us could cut tobacco, he happily invited us to come out and work for him. He would take us on weekends when we didn't have a meet and hold an informal cross-country camp where we would camp out in his barn, do a long run in the morning, and then work the rest of Saturday at the various tasks of putting a tobacco crop in the barn.

The bonus for us was that he had a basketball hoop set up in his barn and he didn't seem to mind if we wanted to stay up and play ball until late into the night.

One weekend late in August, we would lay sticks and clean up the barn in preparation for housing the tobacco. When the tobacco was ready, we would cut and house the tobacco crops from the various farms. This was hard work, but it paid pretty well compared to other jobs we could get.

When we were finished with his crops, he would recommend us to other farmers he knew who needed to hire some help.

This kind of work always appealed to me because it was the kind of job where you could see the progress you were making just by watching the long rows of tobacco plants shrink. It was hot and dirty work, which when done in a friendly spirit of competition, gave me a lot of satisfaction. You can't hurry beyond the point of doing the job right, but it goes a lot better when you know if you slack off, the other cutters will be further up the row. The same people who were good at this work were also likely to be pretty good athletes, the kind who wouldn't quit or give up when things got tough.

When the tobacco was all cut and housed, it was usually time for the big cross-country meets – the late season invitationals, Regionals, and State. Later in the fall when the season was over, we would get hired to strip tobacco which was also tedious and dirty work but it was another chance to get together away from school and training and hear some great stories from the older farmers and people who would gather in the tobacco stripping rooms. Jim's dad, Rueben, was an icon of the Northern Kentucky education community, and even in his 70's could put in a full day working right along with us and critiquing the work we did. After one particularly hard day, which was made worse by delays over equipment frustrations, and ending when it got too dark to work anymore, Gerry Baynun slouched in the backseat as we sleepily rode home and said, "I just got outworked by a 75 year old man."

Several of my other friends also owned farms and were glad to have a crew for the seasonal work required of family farming. I didn't save much money, but this extra cash came in handy for running shoes, gas, and an occasional record that I wanted to buy.

It seemed even more important to me to build up some cash for this last year, because I was looking forward to visiting some colleges and hoping to get down to Lexington where my girlfriend was attending the University of Kentucky.

Between my regular job, running, and farm work, I almost never had a spare moment until school started. Class time was my best opportunity to sit still and let my body rest and recover. I slept like a baby at night and I always functioned well on less sleep than most people need, but I liked the sitting still part of class.

Since I had accumulated enough credits and had a few good teacher recommendations, I was allowed to participate in a co-op program for my senior year. When school started, I would have three classes in the morning and then I was released from school to walk the half mile to the highway, before getting on the Transit Authority of Northern Kentucky bus for the ride north down the highway to Redwood School and Rehabilitation Center. My "co-op" consisted of tutoring disabled and otherwise disadvantage kids in Math and English. My supervisor at the school was young and, as I would learn, very good at her job. She must have made a quick assessment of me and determined I was up to the task because she put me right to work helping a half dozen students with their math homework problems. In the beginning I was hesitant, not having been taught the first thing about how to teach. But as the year went along, I gained confidence and developed relationships with each of the kids who looked forward to having me come in to the classroom. I don't know who learned more: them for the one-on-one extra help I was giving them, or me for the greater appreciation I gained for the gift of my comparatively high functioning brain and body.

JUGGERNAUTS

Before Redwood dismissed their students, I had to leave in order to catch the bus back down the highway to make it to cross-country practice. It usually worked out exactly right if I got off the bus and jogged the half mile from the highway to school. I would run into the locker room and change from my jeans into my running shorts and head outside to stretch with my teammates.

I hate a parade. Everything about them. My earliest memory of beginning to hate parades comes from having the privilege of marching in the Memorial Day Parade through Erlanger in my little league baseball uniform, when I was maybe 8 years old. The uniforms in the 1960's definitely classified as old school – they were made of 100% wool flannel, not the slick nylon polymers of to-day's comfortable sportswear. You've seen the pictures of Ty Cobb in 1907 – ours looked just like that. They sat in the basement of the church all winter to capture the smell of must and mildew, and probably were no less than fifteen years old by the time they got to us. Mine, I am sure, was way too large which meant I had it doubled up on me somewhere. I loved to play baseball so much I didn't even notice the hot uniform when I put it on to play in games, but Memorial Day came around and it was always over ninety degrees when the parade started at 10:00 a.m.

Our baseball coach considered it an honor to be asked to march his team in the parade, but even at eight I wondered what honor was in it when every other team in the league was marching too. Even the ones we could beat. Along with all the local Boy Scout troops, the school's marching band in their dark, made-for-fall uniforms (at least our wool baseball uniforms had started out being white), and hosts of other dignitaries all of whom had absolutely nothing to do with Memorializing anything would walk along the parade route at a pace so slow the chewing gum I stepped in would glue my sneakers to the hot pavement. Maybe I was just too impatient for my own good, but I was from a generation of kids who obediently did what they were told to do by adults so I marched in the parade.

Along this very same parade route on Dixie Highway, there is an intersection with Cowie Avenue which is two blocks from Lloyd Memorial High School. Such an intersection had the types of establishments you would expect to have with the kind of traffic passing by it: a pizza parlor, a movie theater, a funeral home, and a public library. This general vicinity was a great place to hangout, and teenagers from all over the community would gather there in the evenings. It was at this intersection where there occurred an historic event some nine years after my first Memorial Day parade.

Over the years it has come to be known as the "The Big One" by those who participated and is often remembered with an "Oh. My. God!" by those who only watched. Those who missed it say they would give anything to have seen it (and a great many people who weren't there claimed to have been). Those who witnessed it say they will never be the same for having done so.

Everyone who was young in the 1970's remembers a song entitled "The Streak" which went something like this: "Oh yes they call him the streak, the fastest thing on two feet . . ." This was the part of the song I liked best, but it goes on to tell the story of some famous streaker running unclothed through the streets of his community. The song may have had a triggering effect, but the real credit or blame--depending on your point of view-- goes to the entire cross-country team, of which I was a member.

Streaking was gaining popularity on college campuses across America in the early 1970's, but the streaking the college kids did was rudimentary compared to the version we evolved in our running careers. Their gauche style usually involved one guy who was so ashamed of his running form he wore a stocking cap over his face to disguise his identity. They would don their masks and run naked, though incognito, through a cafeteria or across the campus in the dark, and then I don't know what they would do.

In other words, theirs was an individual sport. This always seemed a little weird to us. We thought of streaking as a team sport and when gender equity issues came up, which they did with great regularity in the mid 1970's, we sincerely hoped our school board would vote to field a women's team too.

Our idea of streaking was considerably more cutting edge than the college version we had read about. I say read because to my knowledge the television news crews were never able to actually capture a streaker on camera for broadcast, and probably would not have been allowed to air the footage if they had any. There are many finer elements of streaking the casual observer may not be aware of. These had to be practiced, honed to near perfection before you could really call yourself an expert streaker.

First of all, you had to know how to run really fast. Identifying someone who goes by in a split second is considerably more difficult than getting a good look at someone going by slowly or simply standing still. We figured parading around naked slowly was about the same as indecent exposure, which we knew was against the law.

Secondly you needed to know the turf you were going to run. A place where you could dress in private is a lot easier to locate if it is planned in advance than if you simply try to wing it.

And lastly, you had to know darn well for certain that your accomplices would not rat you out if someone was caught by the police or someone's parents.

Streaking, technically speaking, is an illegal act. It probably comes under the subsection of laws having to do with public indecency or lewd and lascivious behavior. The police would probably not have arrested you in 1975 if they caught you red handed (or "white butted" as we frequently said) but there were fates worse than criminal prosecution. In my neighborhood, you had more to fear from your parents than you did the law and the police quickly caught on to this. The cops would load you up and simply take you home knowing for certain justice was sure to follow.

It was not uncommon for a mother to be seen dragging a little kid through the neighborhood by his ear, politely rapping on the door of his house, and begin the prosecution with "Janie, do you know what Jimmy just did? . . ."

Jimmy's mom would take hold of his other ear and thank her neighbor and Jimmy would invariably hear the words a kid fears most from his mother: his full Christian name. And if you had done something really wrong, she would finish with "Wait 'til your father gets home."

It was not much better for the teenage crowd. A parent's wrath could extend to grounding, removing of all driving privileges, and cancellation of any extracurricular activities (which in my case would mean no track or cross-country). I was never caught streaking but I will confess to just this one incident. As it was, I take responsibility only for the premeditated conspiracy to humiliate but was only a secondary accomplice to the actual unlawful act. The story goes something like this:

On the Thursday before our Friday night Homecoming Football Game, our high school put on a town Homecoming Parade featuring the king and queen candidates riding in convertible muscle cars, cheerleaders (the few who were not also queen candidates) in pickup trucks, the marching band, and a few odd dignitaries and school administrators. Usually a couple of football players would spray paint their old nasty pickups in the school colors, load them up with anybody who wanted to ride, and overheat their engines while idling for an hour down Dixie Highway. This ritual probably occurs in every town in America and the glory in it has somehow always eluded me. It probably goes back to my early Memorial Day experiences but that may be over-analyzing it.

The parade ended at the school where a pep rally and bonfire awaited the student population. It was here that I introduced the concept to a few of my teammates. All I really said was "How you getting home?" to Jude.

"We're walking. The Camaro ran out of gas on the way home from school today and we got a ride up here from my sister," he answered.

"Look me up before you leave. Me and Johnny will walk home with you," I said.

My brother John and Jude's brother Beaves were with us and heard our plan. Denny was standing there with that sparkle in his eyes and he started humming "The Streak." We laughed knowing this was his reminder of our previous night's run through town, the last mile or so naked except for our Nikes and our running shorts worn like nun hats on our heads with the elastic waistband over top of our ears. We seldom wore shirts on these very hot night runs, so it was pretty simple to go from runner to streaker.

I overheard Beaves telling a big guy on the football team "I swear!" and the big guy laughed and shook his head. He looked over at the group of us standing there. The big guy said something else I could make out, and then I heard him say he would catch up to the Beaves later and sauntered off laughing and shaking his head.

"Potter says he'd like to streak with us sometime," Beaves announced as he walked over to us, speaking of the big guy who played defensive end on the football team.

"Now that would be something to see!" Johnny said.

A half-hour later, I got the feeling something wasn't quite right. As we wandered around the pep rally, I noticed some of the other guys looking over their shoulders at us, and some of the girls covering their giggles with their hands as they looked at us.

Ten minutes later I knew for certain things were getting out of hand when a girl I knew came up to me and asked "Are you guys really going to do it?"

"Do what?" I asked.

She giggled "Streak across Dixie Highway?"

"Where'd you hear that?"

"Those guys told us," she said and pointed out towards a swelling crowd of football players, local rowdies, and a few of my teammates.

I shrugged my shoulders and headed over to check it out.

"What's going on?" I asked Jude.

"Beaves dared the football team to streak across Dixie Highway," he said as the excitement began to well up inside him. "And we're going with them."

He could hardly contain his enthusiasm.

"They can't keep up with us," I stated as a known fact.

"I know," he said and laughed that peculiar laugh he reserved for particularly hilarious situations. He shook his head in the affirmative and I finally got it.

It was a pretty cruel thing to do and I doubt if the Beaves was really clever enough to think about it in this way, but all of a sudden I was remembering the old joke about the guy taking his track shoes out of his backpack and the guy's camping buddy says "You can't outrun a bear!"

228

"I know," the punch line goes, "but I don't have to if I can outrun you."

When the pep rally ended was when I knew something huge was taking shape. The crowd milled out, but instead of getting into their cars, most of the crowd began walking the half-mile up to Dixie Highway.

I found my brother and the Baynum brothers, Denny, and several more of my teammates. We went out through the gates of the football field and into the parking lot. Within half a block, I looked around and there was a virtual mob of thirty or more guys following us up the street.

The next several minutes remain blurred, even in the blinding light of 20/20 hindsight. The image that keeps coming back to me is of forty sixteen, seventeen, and eighteen year old boys stripping down to their shoes and socks and trying to figure out how to secure their clothes in a bundle small enough to carry at a dead sprint. If there was any plan or organization for what was going to happen next, I could not figure out what it was. We were huddled behind the funeral parlor in the darkened parking lot but there was a fairly well lighted section of Dixie Highway and several hundred assembled spectators within a few hundred feet around the corner from where we stood.

For a very short time I stood there thinking, "There is no way . . ." I could not imagine leading this bunch out from the shelter of the darkness where we stood. For all I could tell there was no one else up to the challenge either. It was a uniquely odd situation: the first one out would stand the greatest risk of giving up their identity while also standing a considerable chance of being the only one to go should everyone else decide this might not be such a good idea after all. While at the same time, the ones bringing up the rear would have the greatest chance of being nabbed from behind or stuck in car traffic. The jostling for ideal

229

position started to occur as soon as everyone got the idea this was really happening. Once somebody took that first step out of the shadows there would be no turning back without a considerable amount of damage to their reputation and ensuing grief they would have to endure most likely for the rest of their life.

As it turned out, someone did step forward. Up through the crowd came the only person ever to play freshman football for our school and weigh three hundred pounds. Not only was this guy Potter huge, but he was the only white guy I have known who could grow a decent afro which just happened to be naturally blond.

"Which way we going?" he asked me for some reason.

"We're following you," I said. What I really meant was "You go ahead and we'll see what happens. But whatever happens, I am going to light the afterburners and whatever bear is chasing us will get a much better meal than he could have from my skin and bones."

Without another word or seeming thought of the consequences, he "Whooped" and broke out ahead of a herd of forty nervous and completely mismatched streakers, each of whom jockeyed for position in the very center of the mass of naked humanity. It was like nothing else I have ever seen. Some of the bodies were the lean and hungry bodies of distance runners while others were the various muscled sizes required for the different positions in football. A swarming fluid mass of pale skin and black skin moving in unison but with a complete reckless abandon toward an undetermined destination.

I must not have been the only one amazed at this sight. Even though it was night, there was enough light from the businesses and sporadic street lights to pretty well see what was going on. Having secured my position somewhere near the front left edge of this herd, I glanced around at the spectators who had gathered at the intersection. We probably could have charged admission judging by the size of the crowd of students who had gotten the short advance notice. I thought everything was going along ok for a few seconds when I noticed the traffic light changing from green to yellow at the intersection just as I started across the highway. Over the fifty yards or so we had run, the swarm began to string out a little and my eye for judging closure was telling me that not everyone was going to make it across the highway before the light changed. It also occurred to me that most of the streakers behind me were lineman and quickly running out of gas.

There were easily a dozen cars stopped in each direction of the four-lane highway.

The occupants of these cars were the real victims of our criminal act. These were all local people on their way home from work or grocery shopping. Chances were good that some of these people were related to some of the naked throng passing before them.

As the light went from yellow to red, I looked up and saw the best course for me to take was the dark alley running toward the railroad tracks which we had to cross to go home anyway. The alley was several blocks long and I knew the route well from many night runs through it. I figured my brother and the Baynums would also figure this out if they didn't actually see me but I slowed down and looked back just as the first couple of cars released their brakes and started forward.

You might imagine that if you were running naked across a major thoroughfare, the last thing you would want to do is stop cold in your tracks. Not only does this increase your chances of being identified but it also limits your already diminished options. Going back is already ruled out. Being run over by a car is not high on the list either, so what happened next was understandable.

As the cars started slowly forward, the tail end of the now fairly strung out pack proceeded through weaving behind and between the slow moving cars. I heard over the next few seconds the following sounds: car horns blown in anger and then just blown for fun, the slap of big hands on the hoods, trunks, and quarter panels of the moving cars, the shouting of drivers out their windows, and the shrieking laughter of the crowd of student spectators. I was laughing so hard myself I was in danger of hyperventilating.

Just as I was coming to a complete stop to see what would happen next, the swarm turned the opposite direction from where I had gone and headed toward a parallel side street. Jude and Johnny came streaking by me and Jude shouted, "Hadley, let's book it!" as he headed down the alley. I wondered what his rush was, but turned and followed him.

I caught up with them and we scampered the quarter mile down the alley to the railroad tracks where we climbed the embankment, crossed the tracks, and went down the other side. We were sheltered from the view of anyone coming down the alley and we quickly dressed and climbed back up to look and see Beaves, Denny, and a couple of others coming down the alley at full speed. We casually stood on the tracks and watched them come up and jump down the other side.

When they joined us on the tracks, we all stood there quietly for several minutes letting our breathing return to normal. In the spirit of not wanting to let on that this short little sprint had winded us in the slightest, we all pretended to be just waiting for the next group to come down the alley. In reality, the short sprint had been a combination of all out effort, competitive adrenaline, and only half-masked fear of being caught at a potentially season ending prank that none of us could have endured – had we been caught.

Maybe it was because I was really a little bit ashamed, or maybe it was just simple modesty, but for whatever reason I did not want to go back to the highway and join the crowd of our fellow students. I knew better than to attempt a mass streak with a bunch of amateurs, let alone rookies, who had no experience in the subtleties of this emerging sport.

I talked John into going home with me and said goodbye to the others who had decided to go back to check it out. When I got home I did some homework and went to bed.

At school the next day, Jude told me his aunt had called his mom the night before and told her about being caught at the light on Dixie when "a hundred naked boys came running over top of the cars." She wondered if Jude and Beaves had said anything about it.

When I got home from school that day, my mom told me she had washed and ironed my dress shirt for the dance. I thanked her and grabbed my laundry basket and bounded up the steps to the bedroom I shared with my three brothers.

When I was putting away my clothes I found the pair of cutoff jean shorts I had worn the night before to the parade, my lucky Speedos still wadded up in the pocket.

STEVE ADKISSON

Kentucky Enquirer 10/3/1975
Cross-Country Winning New Popularity

-Herb Whitney Kentucky Sports

There's a new world dawning. The times they are a'changing.

Translation: Move over, football. There's a new fall sport in town. And people are slowly growing to appreciate it.

It's called cross-country. Once almost strictly a conditioning exercise for basketball players, the ancient art of running has grown to the point in Northern Kentucky where even the football players are taking notice.

So it was at Wednesday's Covington Catholic-Lloyd-Holmes triangular meet that the Covington Catholic football players stopped what they were doing twice to form a welcoming funnel at the finish of the varsity and jayvee races.

"That never happened when I was running cross-country," said Larry Kramer, who used to run at Covington Catholic and now works full time in the bakery supply business with his father and part time in the sportswriting business with me. "When I ran, the football players never left practice during a meet. They didn't pay any attention to us."

At Wednesday's meet, also present were Tim Stein of the Kentucky Post and myself.

Two reporters covering a regular season cross-country meet? Football teams should be as lucky.

"I'm not saying this just because you two guys are here today, but I think last year's cross-country coverage in your two papers really gave the sport a needed impetus to grow," said Lloyd coach Mike Daley. "New teams have

sprung up at Campbell County, Bellevue, and Holy Cross. The interest in cross-country has never been greater around here. With the addition of girls cross-country, the sport is growing like never before"

Jack Kaelin agrees. The Covington Catholic coach has watched the sport grow in his 10 seasons at the Colonel helm. Wednesday's meet over the course he built was a personal highlight.

"This is a great moment for all of us in cross-country," Kaelin said as he pointed to the fans standing on the hilly terrain behind the school. "There have been times as a coach when we've run before no fans at all. Things do seem to be changing."

* * * * *

The reason football has always been autumn's biggest sport is that football is the top money-making sport in high school.

Of course, football makes money because it attracts followers. Most prefer the brutal grace of football over the grueling dogged-ness of cross-country.

Cross-country makes no money. Hence, school officials usually aren't intensely interested in promoting it. But men like Kaelin and Daley and Charlie Jenkins of Holmes have created their own athletic worlds by training and developing runners of the first order.

* * * * *

The fact that cross-country brings in no hard cash may not be such a drawback.

"It's absolutely the cheapest sport to organize," Daley said. "We use the same uniforms that we use in track. And

you really don't need uniforms. Kids could run in shorts and T-shirts if they wanted.

"The shoes are the only expense, and our runners at Lloyd pay for their own, often buying them for $5 a pair in the ads for factory rejects in the back of Runner's World."

Football, while it brings in the money, also costs a bundle to run. It is far and away the most expensive sport in high school.

"A runner is accepted more now," Daley said. "We've had some good American distance runners in recent years and that has helped create interest.

"In our locker room we've got pictures all over the place of Frank Shorter (1972 Olympic marathon champion) and Steve Prefontaine (one of the world's most versatile distance men before his death in an automobile accident recently). It adds something. The kids love it.

"We had to take the money out of our own pockets to buy the pictures, but it was worth it."

Senior year in high school is meant to be a time of demonstrating how ready a person is for taking on the real world. College plans have to be made and the appropriate steps taken to get there. Some people who have aspired to a trade are looking forward to getting out into the working world and finally making some money. For some, marriage is the next step after fulfilling promises to parents that they will wait until after graduation.

For some reason though, I seemed to have regressed from a maturity standpoint from where I'd been the year before. I had less confidence and was much more uncertain about what I would do when I got out of school. Some of this had to do with having put so much energy into running for my first three years in school. All I had cared about was what I was good at, which was running. I was sure of my future course because I was going to get a running scholarship to one of the schools that had great running programs like Western Kentucky, Oregon, or the University of Kentucky.

When the injury came, I was forced to take a hard look at my realistic opportunities to go to college. For quite a while I pretty much decided I would just get a job when I graduated from high school and do whatever life might have had in store for me. This was a decision made from feeling sorry for myself, and had more to do with pride than frustration. It took so long for my leg to get better that I had let all the negative thoughts creep back in – thoughts like "I'll never get back in the kind of shape I was in before," and "If I can't run well, I would rather not put myself in a position where I lose." It took a while to dig myself out of this kind of thinking.

I had a lot of help from my teammates. Since most of any kind of success is due to the attitude you bring with you, it was no wonder the Juggernauts were so good. Jude and Gerry Baynum are two of the most positive, never-say-quit people you are likely to ever run across. My brother John has a remarkable capacity for summarizing complicated emotional situations and finding just the right thing to say, in as few words as possible to make his point. He encouraged by what he did more than by what he said. Coach Daley gave encouragement to every athlete he came in contact with and had the ability to lead and motivate. My mother, especially, was gifted with a saintly touch to sooth and inspire when things weren't right.

Sport is supposed to be fun and we were masters at this aspect of teamwork.

There was never a day that went by without some joke, or stunt, or revelation, making the entire team laugh hysterically. When things got dull, Jude could bring a smile by giving his "Laugh of Death" which I can only describe as the loudest, most unique method of expressing joy that I have ever heard.

Whenever Jude wanted your attention while he was doing, or about to do, a visual stunt, he would give out this laugh. On his regular trips to the Gatorade machine located outside the locker room in the parking lot, dressed only in the towel he'd wrapped around his body after taking a shower, he would give the laugh and half the team would roll on the floor. This laugh became one of our standard huddle break calls because it was so strange that the other teams could never figure out what could have been so funny to cause someone to laugh like that. The laugh itself was what made the rest of us laugh, almost to tears sometimes, as we stumbled out of our huddle and jogged back to the starting line with the kind of bounce only joy can bring.

Several recurring superstitions developed over my last cross-country season.

Each summer, Erlanger has a big carnival which included one of those traveling gypsy circuses. The Lions Carnival was held at the Erlanger Lions complex of baseball fields which was in the path of many of our running courses. One day, just after the circus left town, as we ran through the complex, I found an elephant turd which had been shoveled out of the pen and thrown out into the grass. I jogged back to the school carrying the dry turd which was the size and general shape of a softball and had the consistency of dried alfalfa hay. I stashed in my locker, half expecting it to stink up the whole place but I guess it was dry enough to have released all the stink before I acquired it.

For some strange reason, I ran well the next day without any pain in my hamstring and I simply put two and two together to come up with the idea that the turd was good luck. It stayed in my locker for the entire season and I bestowed it upon my brother after graduation.

JUGGERNAUTS

Our team had retained our same rituals in preparing for race day – walking the course, jogging two miles, listening to Led Zeppelin's "Stairway To Heaven," sitting in a circle doing butterfly and other stretches while we sang inane songs, strideouts, huddle, prayer, joke, huddle break, race. But we also developed new routines throughout the training week which had the same flavor as far as being considered necessary for the right mojo when race day came around. One of my individual idiosyncrasies was a favorite pair of jeans I managed to wear every single day of my senior year. My mother was meticulously clean and even though I did actually own two or three pairs of pants, I managed to get my favorite ones into the laundry on a regular enough basis that she never caught on. My "school" jeans did not really get that dirty because I only wore them to class, to my teaching co-op, and after that I ran around in running clothes for most of the rest of the evening.

Even with all the extraneous aspects of preparing for competition, we knew deep down that we would have to take care of our business when the gun went off. In our first meet of the season, I felt better than I'd felt in a long time. I managed to win in 10:09 on our home course and our team scored just twenty points to beat our local rival Dixie. I had run five miles before school that day.

It surprised me to win this race because Jude had been so strong and had easily beaten me in Charleston as well as in most of our hard practice intervals. I must have caught him napping or else he must have had an off day because after this first race he dominated the middle part of the season. He won all of our dual meets finishing ahead of me in the few big meets he didn't win, often setting new course records.

Jude and I continued to duel it out over all the courses where we had raced together for the prior three seasons. The

239

races took on a very similar feel to the year before with the two of us running away from the field early and then eventually Jude would get just enough of a lead over me that I would realize I wasn't going to catch him. Each time out I fought and competed until there was nothing left in the tank. I tried various strategies such as holding back early and then making a big run in the middle but by then Jude was already out of reach. I tried to simply run away from Jude from the gun, which was extremely painful for me later in the race when Jude would easily run away from me. No matter what I threw at him, he was able to take it and then add a little more. Probably better than anyone else in the wide, wide world of sports, Jude knew what it felt like to be me. I had done the same thing to him for the whole previous year.

Our teammates were making amazing progress and I honestly believe if coach would have held Jude and me out of meets, our next seven runners would have won all of the meets without us. In many of the smaller meets, it was almost like there were two races: the one between Jude and me and then the one between our three through seven runners and the other teams' one through five runners. Our team strategy was to place our 7th runner ahead of the opponents 5th runner. Although somebody later worked the math out to disprove the theory, at least in larger meets, Coach Daley had ingrained the thought into our heads that we could not lose if we did this. He was as proud of our ability to accomplish this team goal of putting our 7th runner ahead of their 5th runner as he was about anything else we accomplished in the meets.

Somewhere during this stretch of finishing second to Jude, I started to accept the fact that doing my very best and not winning was not the same as losing. For a hyper-competitive person, this was a big step. Accepting and embracing my place as part of a very good team made the season a lot more fun and me a lot more fun to be around. I realized I had to continue to train and dig deep everyday to make myself better. The goal was to make sure I was ready to give my very best each time out – even if my very best was not going to put me on the top podium step. Racing a lot, as we did, gave me ample opportunity to experience this new form of acceptance. Other than the early season victory, I finished 2nd place to Jude in each of our next seven meets.

In the middle of October, Jude was out one meet with the flu and I won in exactly the same time I had run on our home course the week before when I had finished twenty yards behind Jude. It was somehow fortuitous that Jude missed this last home meet we would ever run on the familiar course and although I knew he could and would have beaten me had he run, I immensely enjoyed running alone at the head of the pack on the very last lap of our home course. Several of my senior friends who were not runners had come out to watch us run this last meet. It was one of many emotional moments I would experience over the next few weeks when I finished and came through the chute to find a long line of family, friends, and former teammates clapping and cheering.

When I finished, shook hands and accepted hugs from my mom and dad, I jogged backwards around the course cheering on my teammates. When my brother John and Gerry Baynum came around, I took an extra long look at them as they finished side by side knowing it was the last time I would ever see them run this stretch of our home course.

When the race was over and the crowd left, Coach Daley brought the team together to go over the details of the last weeks of the season. The only meets remaining were the Conference Meet, the Regional Championship which would determine the teams that went to State, and then the State Meet which was to be held two weeks after the Regional on the campus of the University of Kentucky.

After our fairly easy victory in the dual meet, even without our best runner, Coach had decided on a new and unusual setup for our Conference Meet which would be held the following Monday, just five days before the Regional. Since there were several extremely strong young runners on our Junior Varsity, and several seniors who were not in our top seven, Coach decided to break with his own rule. He was going to let the seniors compete on the varsity in the Conference and let two Juniors – Jeff Ogden and Dennis McCracken duel it out in the JV race to see who would get to be the seventh runner on the varsity team. Jeff had been the seventh man consistently, but Dennis had come on strong late in the season and had actually run a faster time in the last JV race than Jeff had in the varsity race. As Coach had clearly described before the season started, we were going with the best seven and the only way to fairly decide this was to let them race head to head. This meet would also give Jeff a chance at winning individually which was something he had not experienced this year as part of the varsity.

Coach gave us another bit of news. He was trying to arrange another practice meet between Regional and State since he did not like the thought of going two full weeks without a race effort. I think most of us agreed with this idea since it would have seemed like an eternity to us to wait two weeks between races.

After this team meeting, most of us went out to do an easy five miles. It was a strangely quiet run. There was a lot to think about and each of us were rerunning the race in our minds and looking ahead to what the next few weeks would bring.

JUGGERNAUTS

Go Ask Alice
Homecoming

-<u>The Tatler</u>, Volume IV 1975

Barely a year ago, Australopithecus aferensis was discovered in Ethiopia. This hominid that lived between 3.9 and 3 million years ago is a newly discovered link between previous versions of upright walking species and the modern Homo sapiens on display in all its hubristic immaturity last Thursday night after the Homecoming Parade. I think even "Lucy" would have thought it churlish, and beneath her to use her large brain and ability to cover ground without scraping her knuckles to such a degrading purpose.

What vacuous idiocy is spewing forth from our halls of learning?

We should never have climbed down from the trees.

"Later I perfected the involuted style of bragging about not bragging to such a degree that I became able to brag in reverse, exalting what I couldn't do and didn't have."

-Rob Brezsny

Standing at the starting line for the Conference Meet were the five seniors on the team – Jude, myself, Denny, Doug, and Terry, along with my brother John, a junior, and sophomore Gerry. It was an exciting feeling to have all of the seniors competing together for the last time. Doug had run for two years and Terry had run all four years but the strength and talent of several of the younger runners had left them out of the larger meets. They were both hard workers and would have been in the top five on any other team in the State and I was thrilled to line up with them for the Conference Meet.

The Northern Kentucky Region is divided into several athletic Conferences and unlike basketball and baseball where the Conference Championship determined who advanced to the Regional Tournaments, the Cross-Country Conference meet was just another opportunity to race in a big meet. They did award medals and trophies to the top individuals and teams, but in terms of being important as a step towards the goal of winning the State Championship, it was not a key race. We took it seriously but knew the real racing started at the Regional.

This Conference Meet was being held for the first time on the Summit Hills Golf Course, which was without question the place I had run more miles than any other single place in my four years of running. The golf course was a beautiful large tract of land only about 1 mile from our house and many of my morning runs had been up to the golf course and then one long loop around the perimeter. I don't think the groundskeepers really liked us running there, but since we were usually there at first light and only ran along the outermost perimeter they never really had much of a chance to tell us. And like Gerry often said, "What are they gonna do Hadley, run you down and ask you to leave?"

On many of these runs we would stop and take our shoes off and hide them under some shrubs. Then we ran the 3 mile loop barefooted on the soft newly mowed grass. It was a hilly loop but we enjoyed cruising barefoot over the long stretches of fairway, watching the sun come up.

After going through our team warm up and pre-race rituals, the gun was shot and off we went. Jude, who had fully recovered from the flu, and I took off together and ran side by side over the course. The two of us had run the course the night before using a map Coach had given us and so we pretty much knew what to expect. But since this was the first cross-country race ever at Summit Hills, the course marking was sketchy and several runners went off the marked course.

The course they had laid out was made up of one long loop of about 1 ½ miles and then a second shorter loop of ½ mile. The second loop went through the same area as the beginning of the first and when Jude and I rounded the tree used as the turn marker for the farthest corner, we were surprised to see Doug come running out of the woods right beside us. We could here other voices coming from down in the woods and Doug ran up to us and said "We made a wrong turn."

There wasn't much else for him to do at this point but to join us on our way back to the finish line and I know Coach wasn't the only one who was amazed to see the three of us coming down the finishing straight together.

Jude and I sprinted in to the end with him nipping me at the end with a wide grin and Doug finishing just a few seconds behind us.

The rest of the pack came in at various intervals behind us and it became obvious from the complaints and odd placements of the better known runners that something was amiss. The meet's host officials never did really sort out the finishing places or team scores and in fact debated re-running the entire meet in order to be fair and accurate. I thought this would have been a cool way to resolve the issue, but several of the other teams had buses waiting and it was getting late in the day for starting another race.

Later on we figured out that some runners from Boone County had taken several of the course marking flags out and relocated them, directing the runners into a dead end trail in the woods. Jude and I had gone right past that turn and, since we knew where we were headed, just ignored the marking flags. By the time we came back around, the entire pack had decided they were not on the course and had taken it upon themselves to get back to it the best they could. Doug had used his knowledge of the area to scramble through the woods and come back out on the course at just the right time to rejoin the race at the front. He earned a bronze medal in the Conference Meet and Lloyd was awarded the Conference Team Title. I don't know that they ever decided how to score the meet beyond that.

Jeff Ogden had beaten Dennis McCracken in winning the Junior Varsity race, earning his spot back on to the varsity for the Regional and, hopefully, the State Meets.

JUGGERNAUTS

"in autumn if there are trees eyes will open
one moment of freedom partakes of it all
those who will imitate will betray
the dogs are happy leading the archers
the hunter is hunted the dealer is dealt the listener is heard
the halls of government are the exhibition palaces of fear
anguish rusts
the poor believe that all is possible for others
each fruit hopes to give light
the air is clear as though we should live forever . . ."

from BALLADE OF SAYINGS
-W.S. Merwin

I woke up in the dark, looked at my alarm clock, saw 5:42, and knew I wasn't going back to sleep. I laid there on the bottom bunk in the room I shared with three brothers, the oldest of which was gone to college, and the youngest of which was asleep in the top bunk above me. My brother John was also awake across the room – I could tell by the sounds of his wrapping himself up in his blankets.

After a few minutes to let my body come alive, I sat up, slid my feet around, and placed them on the floor. I looked across the room and could see John's face turned toward me.

"You ready for this?" I said.

"Oh, yeah," came his answer.

We dressed in our team uniforms and put on our sweats and shoes. We went downstairs and our mom was already up in the kitchen getting breakfast ready. She knew we both liked oatmeal on race day and had a pot going with enough for the six of us in the house. I could also smell cinnamon toast coming from the oven.

We ate breakfast and hung around the house for a while, then headed up to the school where we were scheduled to meet at 7:00. True to form, at 6:45, everybody was there and five of us crowded into Jude's Camaro to listen to the radio and get ready to race.

Our Regional race started at 10:40 but for the first time in history, there would be a girl's Regional and we wanted to get there early enough to get a good parking spot and see the girl's race which started at 9:40. There were only a few schools who were able to field teams and I always believed Coach Daley's ability to get the press to cover cross-country had something to do with the growing popularity of the sport. Title IX, which guaranteed equal opportunity for female athletes was a tiny thirty-seven word federal law passed in 1972 and would have an amazing positive effect on women's sports over the next few years. Not since the suffragists' success in the early part of the last century has a single act empowered women more than Title IX. It states simply "No person in the United States shall, on the basis of sex, be excluded from participation in, be denied the benefits of, or be subjected to discrimination under any education program or activity receiving Federal financial assistance." What seemed amazing to me was that they had to write a law. My girlfriend was a runner and I knew many other girls, who, had they been given the opportunity, would have been great athletes as runners.

Coach Daley opened the door to the locker room for us and we went in to use the facilities and get stuff out of our lockers. On each of our lockers was an envelope which Coach had taped to the doors. I opened mine and went to a corner of the locker room to read it. Coach had never been much of a rah-rah type coach because he knew we had ample motivation to perform at our best, and he had never done anything like this before. I got a peculiar feeling that something was up when I opened the envelope and found a simple quote he had typed on a piece of paper: " 'Be more concerned with your character than with your reputation because your character is what you truly are, while your reputation is what others think you are.' John Wooden." I saw the others opening their envelopes and looking at whatever message Coach wanted to convey to them. We each folded our envelopes up and I stashed mine in the bag where I carried my racing spikes.

When everyone was ready, we divided into two cars and headed out towards the Highland Country Club for our Regional Meet. We followed Coach out of the parking lot and purposely delayed ourselves at the stop signs to let him get ahead of us. Among the strongest superstitions we had as a team was that we had to drive the cloverleaf at the interstate before finally getting the car turned in the direction of the meet. Since the Highland Country Club was north of Erlanger, we got on the southbound entrance ramp to I-75, stayed in the exit lane and exited eastbound at the Erlanger exit, remerged into the eastbound traffic and got back on the northbound ramp to finally head north on I-75. The strangest thing about it was that nobody said a word in Jude's car which I was riding in – we just took the "Cloverleaf" as part of the directions for getting wherever we were going.

Once at the golf course, we stayed in the warm cars for a while and watched as the other teams and spectators came, parked their vehicles, and walked out toward the course. We were conserving our energy and trying to stay relaxed as long as possible before we would get out and get warmed up for our race. Eventually, several of the guys decided it was time to get out and go to watch the girl's race. We got out and went to the course to walk it, but were told by one of the course marshals that the course was closed

for now and while some of my teammates went into the
clubhouse to stay warm, Jude and I went back to his car.
We ended up missing the girls race altogether but I was
really more interested in readying myself to race that being
a spectator anyway. When Jude and I were alone for this
time in his car, we sat silently for a long time.

"You all right?" Jude asked me.

"Yeah, I'm fine. Just thinking about last year when we
beat each other up over here. Man, what was that all about
anyway?"

"Hell Hadley, I don't even remember," he laughed.

"Me neither."

We both knew that we were each other's only competition in this race and we both looked at it as something entirely different from the State Meet where there was
competition aplenty for either of us. The State Meet was
more of an "us against them" proposition and in anything
like that, we didn't even look at it as competition between
us.

The Regional was the last of this "me versus you" racing we would ever do and both of us knew it would be important for the confidence we would take into the State
Meet.

Jude had been recruited by several colleges and knew
there would be several coaches checking up on how well he
ran today. I already knew from experience the thrill of winning a big meet and was determined to have that feeling
again. I had felt very good at practice over the last few
weeks and our times in interval workouts indicated we
were in even better shape than we had been for last year's
Regional when I had run 9:18 and Jude 9:19. I had a feeling
today's race was going to be one last amazing duel between
us and I could tell Jude was feeling the same way. We were
both relaxed, neither of us was sick or injured, and Coach

Daley's knack for getting us to peak at the right time was evident in the confidence we each felt in our abilities to do the best we could.

After our long warm-up and pre-race rituals, our team stood in the starting gate. Jude, myself, and John lined up in the front, and the other four huddled tight right behind us. We gave each other an encouraging nod, while several of the other teams leaned over and wished us good luck. We had taken on another pre-race habit of waiting for this to happen. Gerry looked around at all of us with that supercilious grin, shaking his head, and quietly announced that "Luck's got nothin to do with it."

This was just the exact final component we needed to drive home the mantra we had of Coach Daley's famous saying "This ain't gonna be no pushover, fellas." It cranked the already high competitive spirits up in every one of us.

Bang! The race began pretty much the same as the previous year's Regional. The only difference was there were several other runners, including my brother John, Gerry, and several of the Holmes and Covington Catholic runners going out very hard over the long downhill which started the Highland's Country Club course. The other teams' coaches had given their highly motivated teams instructions to go out hard – something they had learned by racing us over the last few years. Anyone who was a senior racing for a team not likely to go to State knew this could be their last high school race ever and were approaching it that way. John and Gerry were in phenomenal shape and had also peaked at the right time to do their best now that the races really meant something.

This new competitive element added an excitement to the race that brought out the best in all of us. Jude glided easily along, waiting for the right time to make his big move and I was content to run a half step back of the leading pack, conserving my energy for the long uphill I knew was coming at the end of both laps, where I planned to accelerate. With several other runners joining the pack, and with our finely tuned sense of pace, I could tell we were going very fast, but somehow it felt easier with a big group pushing the pace.

When Jude started a long surge just as we started up the hill to complete the first of two laps, I was the only one who was able to move with him. We came to the one mile mark and Coach called out our mile split of 4:32. This was faster than either of us had run the year before and I could tell Jude was still running easily. I was laboring but felt like I could still go hard for another mile.

My favorite photo of our high school cross-country careers is one of Jude and me coming around the first mile of this race. In the black and white photo, we are both in deep concentration, looking effortless, side by side. Neither of my feet is on the ground. We are both wearing the same Nike spikes and dark tee shirts under our Lloyd uniforms.

Steve Adkisson & Jude Baynum at 1975 Regional Meet.
Author collection. Photographer unknown.

When we started back around for the second lap, I glanced back over my shoulder and could see John, Gerry, and Denny well up in the pack that followed us by forty or fifty yards.

One of the few times I thought of using a different strategy besides my standard "run as hard as possible for as long as possible" came to me when I started the second lap. I purposely backed off the pace to let Jude gain a few yards. I thought Jude would welcome the chance to slow down a little and still stay ahead while reserving energy for the kick he would unleash a few minutes later. I was mistaken.

I fell in behind Jude and was able to keep in contact with him with the hope that he would come back to me as we went uphill over the middle part of the course. He, however, had other ideas. He continued to push the pace harder and with even my best effort to close the gap, he pulled away gradually as we raced over the second mile. Although neither of us really paid that much attention to the course records on cross-country courses (because, as we always said, conditions like mud, rain, wind, and cold weather had an impact on how fast anyone could run a particular course on any given day) Jude would go on to set the fastest time ever on the Highland Heights Country Club course.

Jude won the race running a remarkable time of 9:13 bettering the course record of 9:15 set 11 years earlier (though it was debatable if it was really the exact same course) and beating me by 10 seconds. John finished in a career best 6th in 9:36 and Gerry was 8th in 9:38, while our fifth scorer Denny was 16th in 9:51. Jeff, who ran 9:58 was our 6th scorer, and J.C. who just barely missed breaking 10:00 was 7th runner across the line. They both beat out every other teams' 5th place scorers to drive their scores up. Our team score of thirty-three points was a hard-earned, impressive victory for all seven of us, and the papers would claim this team as one of the all time best high school teams of Kentucky. It was unheard of at the time for a Kentucky team to have six runners capable of sub 10:00 for 2 miles. Since the following year Kentucky changed its cross-country distance to 5K, our team's accomplishment would mark the last time this feat would be completed.

Jude's 9:13 was something we were all proud of. We knew how hard he worked and the sacrifices it took to be in that kind of shape. We, probably more so than any of the spectators or opponents, had immense respect and admiration for what he had done. I was thrilled for him, and excited that I was able to get within five seconds of the 9:18 I had run the year before considering the long absence from running I had endured earlier in the year.

We celebrated this success later that evening at a bonfire party at the Baynum's house. Their mom had moved to a house in the country that overlooked the Ohio River. Over the summer we had gathered driftwood and built a huge pile for some unknown future purpose, and today felt like the right time to set it ablaze.

Most of us were naturally drawn to fires from our years of camping and tending to fires in fireplaces and woodstoves, so to be outside on a cold fall night burning the largest single pile of wood I had ever seen was a lot of fun.

It was always interesting to me that as we got older, when we weren't actually running, we hardly ever talked about running. I'm pretty sure it's because we ran so much and had time then to pretty much cover everything there was to say about it. Running is a fairly simple proposition, but it does take a huge amount of mental and emotional energy to push it to the extreme that we were pushing it. We had learned not to expend energy needlessly away from the task at hand and so hanging out away from running was a completely separate thing.

To somebody new to the group, such as somebody's girlfriend from across town, we were undoubtedly an odd bunch of ragamuffins: half wild and half crazy, hard to understand, shy, and introverted. There were way too many inside jokes and ongoing stories which affected our conversations. As usual, I found myself sitting quietly around the fire with my brother and a few close friends, enjoying the "caveman TV," even while some of the more ambitious among my teammates hit on the girls.

You could almost call it a runner's curse, but like most things that are rewarding, an endurance athlete's work is never done. After an easy Sunday run and long hike in the woods in the afternoon, we showed up for practice the Monday after the Regional expecting to get back at it. Coach had told everybody on the team the Friday before Regional that practice was only mandatory for those who would be running in the State Meet in two weeks, but when I went into the locker room after school I couldn't tell the difference in numbers from any other day of practice. There may have been a few who were gone to basketball tryouts, but virtually every one of the runners on the team was there to join us for whatever workout Coach had devised for us, knowing their racing season was over. I will admit here this was the highlight of my high school career, weird as that may sound. Knowing there were thirty or so runners who respected us enough to endure another two weeks of practice just to be around to support the seven of us representing the school at the State Meet made me proud to be a part of such a group of human beings.

Before heading out for our warm-up, Coach let us know he had organized a practice meet with the other teams and individuals from the Region who would be going to the State Meet. We would have this meet on the Saturday of the coming week. Between now and then, we would have an easy week and then do some tapering workouts the following week to get ready for the State Meet.

I recorded our easy week in my log book:

Oct 27 – 8 miles easy on roads by Airport
Oct 28 – 2 mile warmup, 3 miles continuous, each mile faster than last
Oct 29 – 9 miles hard on cross country course being timed
Oct 30 – warmup; 16 x 440 below 70; felt ok, 3 miles cooldown
Oct 31 – Happy Halloween – 1 mile easy

JUGGERNAUTS

Nov 1 – Meet at CCH (to help keep us in shape?) Ran 10:33 which ain't bad tied with Jude for 1st - lost 27-28 to team of individuals?

The week of the State Meet, we cranked up the speed work and it was an amazing feeling to have the ability to get up on my toes and push out some of the fastest repetitions any of us had ever done. On the Monday after the practice meet, John wore his Army boots to the Devou Park hill workout where we did 24 x 200 uphill at the amphitheater. John did it in his heavy boots. I know he believed it helped build his strength for racing but it also had a much bigger effect on the rest of us to know we had someone on our team who was ready, willing, and able to endure this kind of punishment in the interest of preparing himself for a race. I put a big star in my training log by this day and simply stated: *Warmup, 24 x 200 (33-34) at amphitheater hill. John wore Army boots.*

This mild notation doesn't do justice to the effect that witnessing this workout had on the team. While each of us struggled to keep our times in the goal range of thirty-three to thirty-four seconds wearing either our lightest training flats or, in some cases, racing spikes, John was determined to do this workout with the handicap of wearing boots we knew weighed at least two pounds each. He had to work much harder because of the boots, but was somehow able to keep up with the main pack of runners.

Coach Daley did not say a word when John showed up at the park wearing the polished leather high top boots. None of the rest of us remarked on it either, silly as he looked, basically just ignoring one of the typical displays of determination and hard-headedness which was standard operating procedure for this bunch of people.

STEVE ADKISSON

"He who attacks must vanquish, while he who
defends must merely survive."

-Master Po from Kung Fu

There is a finality unlike anything you can imagine in
lining up for the last cross-country race of your senior year
in high school. After four years of buildup and growing
from being a boy to becoming a man, the emotions of the
senior runners can have a tremendous impact on the outcome of the race.

I remembered the State Meet from the year before when
Matt, Steve, and Dave had given their all in their last race.
We had talked about it before and since, and even with
their advice and guidance, I was not prepared for how I felt
in the last few days before the meet. For reasons I cannot
explain I became incredibly nervous and had butterflies like
I hadn't had since the first year or so of racing. I had trouble sleeping and had phantom aches and pains which whit-
tled away at my confidence over the Wednesday and
Thursday before the meet.

After literally hundreds of races - counting track events,
road races, and cross-country, I had eventually become
skilled at controlling my emotions leading up to a big race.
My yoga practice had helped me develop relaxation meth-
ods that worked for even the most stressful situations. But
for whatever reason, I had blown up my expectations for
myself in this, my final high school race, well beyond a
healthy level.

After two virtually sleepless nights, I skipped the football pep rally on Thursday night and stayed home in my
room trying to rest and relax. I finally crashed early and
slept like the dead from 8:00 p.m. or so until my brother

258

woke me at 6:00 on Friday morning to go for an easy run.

After school and a brief team meeting, we drove to Lexington (after negotiating the cloverleaf, of course). Those of us in the car – Jude, Denny, Gerry, John, & myself – were fairly subdued as we headed south on I-75 for the one hour drive. Jude had been sick with a head cold and flulike symptoms most of the week and had skipped a couple of days of practice, but claimed to be feeling much better.

About fifteen miles south of Erlanger there is a Southern Railroad trestle spanning the interstate a good hundred feet above the highway. As we neared the trestle, we could see a large sign fluttering from the top. When we got closer we were craning our necks to get a view of what the sign said. At about the same time, we could each make out the "Take State, Go Juggs!" which somebody had painted in large blue letters on a full size sheet, climbed up the side of the freeway, walked out on the trestle and tied to the two top corners to the guardrails on the railroad overpass. When I say somebody, I would have to suspect it was a couple of guys from Boone County who had stayed up late (or got up early) and gone to the trouble of climbing an extremely dangerous bridge to place the sign.

Aside from the people with me in the car, I could not imagine who would have done it. But knowing that somebody else besides us was capable gave me great hope for the future of the program.

Jude let out one of the most heartfelt "laughs of death" I had ever heard and I don't think any of us stopped laughing for a good five minutes. That pretty much sent half my butterflies fluttering away to wherever they go to hide when we don't need them.

The rest of the short trip took on the flavor of any other occasion when the five of us would be riding around in a car. Jude and Gerry argued and teased each other. Denny egged them on. John and I sat back and laughed while the stereo blared out Jethro Tull and Pink Floyd.

When we pulled up to the huge football stadium parking lot where we were to meet up with Coach and the rest of the team, we were relaxed and enjoyed a casual jog around the course. It was muddy from several days of rain, so we only did the entire course one time.

Coach walked over to where we were wiping the mud off our shoes onto the curb behind Jude's car and we chatted a few minutes. He had already given us the itinerary of when we would head to the hotel, where we were going for supper, and who was rooming together. When we had finished cleaning up our shoes, we loaded back up into the cars and headed across town to our hotel.

After dinner, we retired to our rooms. Remembering how we had suffered in my first State Meet from not sleeping the night before the race, I had let everyone on the team know I was going to have my lights out at 9:00. We were all on the same page I guess, because Jude, John, and Denny who were in my room all laid down at the same time and went right to sleep.

In the morning, Denny and I slipped out the door early and made our away to the outdoor pool which amazingly still had water in it. In the interest of waking ourselves up fully for the day's events, we stripped down to our boxers and made a quick swim across the pool and then ran shivering back to our room. It couldn't have been forty degrees but we were both wide awake and ready for whatever was going to happen.

We woke John and Jude and by the time we were all dressed in our uniforms and packed up, the others and Coach were waiting for us in the parking lot. We stopped at the restaurant and ate a light breakfast and then headed back over to the UK campus.

I was thrilled to see among those standing in the parking lot, Steve Nienaber, who was attending UK and lived literally right across the parking lot from where we were standing.

Coach had already picked up our team's race numbers and handed them out to us. He seemed nervous and a little more protective of us than was normal, but after some warnings to not run around too much and stay close enough to see what was going on, gave his permission for us to walk the course and then go up to Steve's dorm room to use the bathroom and hang out for a while before our race.

The course was a pretty good spectator course with a few decent hills in it, but not nearly as hilly as we would have liked. It did a giant loop around the still undeveloped end of the campus and there were a few trees and a slick gulley crossing on the back side.

John had been unusually secretive about a project he was working on in our basement over the last week. As we got to a secluded part of the course and several of us dashed into the woods to relieve ourselves, he got a chance to show us what he had been working on. Out of his small gym bag where we knew he kept his spikes (but were wondering why he was walking the course carrying), he pulled out another paper bag which he knelt over and used his body to shield us from. When he had finished whatever preparations he was making he waived us all over. There on the ground was a miniature plaster of Paris statue of the Sphinx which he had hollowed out and packed full of our dad's black powder used in reloading shotgun shells. He had attached an Este's model rocket fuse and as he walked away he rolled out the wire which was hooked up to his battery powered rocket launcher. When he estimated we were far enough away to avoid lethal injury, he knelt back down and set the launcher on the grass.

"10, 9, 8, 7 . . ."

"Wait wait wait," Gerry was laughing, but was curious about something.

"What the heck is THAT?" he asked.

"I call it Hedda," John replied. "3, 2, 1."

Hiss, BOOM, laugh of death. Run like hell away from here.

There was probably not a living soul for a mile around who hadn't heard the explosion which was probably the equivalent of a ¼ stick of dynamite and which left nothing but a large cloud of white vapor behind the sound which several thousand sets of ears were trying to locate the source of.

Fortunately for us, we had used our uncanny ability to select a good out-of-view site for such stunts, and as we rounded the back of the stadium to come back into the view of the crowd, all any of the meet officials and coaches saw was our team in a group slow jog looking at the ground ten feet in front of us. No one could notice John was coiling the igniter wire as we jogged along.

So much for butterflies.

With about an hour and half to wait for our race since there were both girls and boys Class A races ahead of our Class AA race, we went up to the dorm in the Kirwin Towers to Steve's room. We cranked up the stereo in the room and lay around on the floor stretching and checking our spikes. Jude mentioned that he wasn't feeling so good and laid down on the bed with his eyes closed. I could not tell if he was genuinely ill or if he was just getting the common upset stomach associated with pre-race jitters. It was great to visit with Steve, but the butterflies were starting to come back in me and I struggled to contain them. By the time everyone took their turn in the restroom, it was pretty much time to head back down to the course to start our warm-up.

As usual, we arrived early to the area where we had arranged to meet up with Coach Daley. He was glad to see us and had his usual excitement and enthusiasm at a higher level than I had ever seen it before. He asked if everyone had everything they needed and how everyone was feeling. Jude told him he was feeling kind of queasy and Coach said to go ahead and warm up and then check back in with him.

We went out to run the course as soon as the last of the runners from the previous race were out of site. The marshals said it was okay to be on the course while the race was going on as long as we stayed behind anyone competing.

While we jogged around, I could tell that Jude was struggling. I felt a brief sense of panic thinking he might end up having the same kind of race at State that Steve had the year before, but knowing that even at a fraction of his capabilities, Jude was going to be able to help the team. As our number one runner, and also as a senior, Jude knew the importance of his contribution. Knowing how mentally strong he was, I knew there was nothing short of a nuclear bomb that would keep him from placing high in the pack.

Wildlife biologist say that in wolf packs, each member of the pack checks with the alpha wolf every single day to make sure the alpha is up to the task of leading the pack. Each subservient wolf is equipped to take over if necessary, and the survival of the pack depends on one of them being willing and capable of taking over.

But what is less commonly known is that when they check and the alpha wolf demonstrates its continued ability to lead, each member of the pack is actually relieved to know they won't have to be the one having their heads kicked in by an elk or bison that day.

As we warmed up, I felt amazingly strong. The strength I had gained from the training and racing through the fall, along with a well designed taper had sharpened my body for the peak performance we had planned for this day. I could sense the same kind of bounce and excitement in the rest of the team. Even Jude perked up as we finished our strides and heard the second call to the starting line.

We stripped out of our sweats and piled them behind our starting gate. In keeping with tradition, we did a long run out about a hundred yards from the starting line and huddled out on the grass.

By this time, I was too excited even to feel like I could say the few unctuous words I had mentally rehearsed. I had planned to tell my teammates how much they meant to me, how amazingly fortunate I was to be able to compete alongside the funniest, stubbornest, hardest working, most dedicated athletes in the world. I wanted to mark this occasion as the one time I was going to come out of my shell and verbalize all the things that I had never said to them.

But that's not the way it worked out. What I ended up doing after we joined hands in the center of the circle and prayed, and while everyone looked to me for some last words of inspiration, was say:

"Close your eyes for a second."

Everyone did.

I could feel my heart pounding inside my chest. I could hear in the distance the murmuring excitement of the crowd, a couple of teams chanting, some band back at the start playing a school fight song.

I could hear the still rapid breathing from my teammates from the run out and warm-up. I could sense the excitement and adrenaline in all seven of us, the pureness of our intentions, however misguided our various and sundry paths to this moment had been. I could still feel the fun in

264

our sense of the unknown outcome of what the next ten to twelve minutes might bring. I felt the conscious willfulness to consider this a battle and a willingness to pay whatever price it would take to know we had left it all out on the course.

"That's what I'm talking about . . . ."

Some things go without saying.

"Juggernauts on three," Jude finally said when the starter hollered out the third and final call for the start.

"Juggernauts!" we all shouted and Jude let out a passable "Laugh of Death."

We jogged back to the starting line. My mind raced with the many thoughts that fill it in the moments before a race. Several of my friends had reminded me of Pre's statement that "A race is a work of art,' and I appreciated that and understood how a running event could be a performance in the sense that a runner could give his all in much the same way as a painter could give his all. But I had a clipping of the full quote in my training log. It reads: "A race is a work of art that people can look at and be affected by in as many ways as they're capable of understanding." Somehow I think Pre was saying that few others could completely understand or conceive of what it is like for him to do what he did. I shared this view. I knew that from here on out, it was really up to me to do whatever it was in me to do, no matter how anyone watching would perceive what I did.

I ran through several possible race scenarios and how I was prepared to respond to each. In scenario one, which was the one I had been counting on and planning for over the last week, Jude would take the lead and everyone else including me would try to hang on for as long as possible. But now that I was aware Jude was not 100%, I envisioned what might happen if he struggled early and the other top runners hung on to his slower pace until later in the race when they had planned a big attack. If this is the way the race panned out, I would not be able to kick with several of the other top runners at the very end of the race.

Johnny Jones had won the previous two State Championships but had graduated, leaving the field open to just a handful of known aspirants to his title. Jude had finished second and I had finished third last year. Right behind me in that race was a tall strong runner from Daviess County named Billy Moorman, who I had beaten this year in the one invitational we had competed against each other in. Several other runners from Lexington and Owensboro were extremely capable of breaking away and winning. There were many unknowns in trying to make a race strategy that could be planned in advance.

In scenario two, I envisioned some over-excited sophomore acting the fool, as Coach would say, and taking the pace out to an insane first mile. This would spread out the field and leave the big kickers struggling to keep up. I hoped something like this would happen because no matter what, I had made up my mind that I was going to hang with the leader as long as possible and I was not going to take the lead until and unless I believed I could hold it to the finish. I had so little confidence in my finishing speed that I knew I would have to build enough of a lead on the kickers in the middle part of the race that they just gave up in the last few hundred yards.

Of course, mentally rehearsing these scenarios was just a habit I had developed as part of my overall approach to being mentally prepared. Most of the actual decisions about race tactics I learned from the experience of many races. There is really no other way to learn these things. You have to expect the unexpected and be prepared to respond to whatever happens.

What usually happens in a race, though, was that you just go out and wing it, because that's all you can really do once the gun goes off and any of a nearly infinite number of possible situations is presented. Just having the awareness of who was around you, assessing their strength or weakness on a given day at various junctures of the race, measuring that against how I felt and where I was in a race – all of this was something experienced at a gut level in a second by second analysis performed subconsciously.

The Juggernauts at starting line at University of Kentucky 1975 State Championship. Denny Heidrich, Jim Clayton, Jeff Ogden, Gerry Baynum, Jude Baynum, John Adkisson. Steve Adkisson stretching. Coaches Jim Hinsdale and Mike Daley standing behind team.

Knowing all this, and being completely prepared and inspired, I was still somehow taken by surprise when the gun went off. Suddenly, the long line of teen warriors had been unleashed upon the world. I am always amazed at the wildness of a mass start at a cross-country race. There were elbows flying, feet stepped on, and a general chaos in the first few hundred yards as the pack fought to be favorably placed at the end of the funnel where the course narrowed to about five yards wide.

For some reason, our entire team got out to a slow start and was boxed in behind a fairly large pack of maybe forty runners at the point where the course narrowed. So much for everyone keying off of Jude.

Glancing around, I saw that all seven of us were still in a tight group – we could have literally touched each other – after the first quarter mile. We had nowhere to go really, with the bottleneck of runners right ahead of us and the course marking tape on both sides. Jude was running right beside me and I could tell he was anxious about moving up from where we were. Even sick, he had enough pride and competitive fire to know we needed to get going pretty soon, or the lead runners would start spreading out the field leaving us too much ground to make up over the last half when the course would open up.

Just a few hundred yards further along, the course made a big sweeping right hand turn and the course marking tape was only set up on the inside of the turn. The left side was open but there was a berm and a ditch there which the course designers figured would act as a natural marker for the course. I was running the inside tangent through the turn when I saw Jude move left and get up on the berm and start accelerating around the outside of the runners ahead of us. I jumped in behind him and over the next hundred yards, we had made our way to the very front of the pack. This big acceleration had seemed fairly easy to me, and I could tell as we went by the big group of runners that they were already slowing somewhat from the extremely fast start of the race.

Now that we were out on the course there were not many spectators, and the only sounds were the breathing of the runners and swishing of our nylon shorts as we hammered along. In the lead pack was Jude, myself, Billy Moorman, a runner from Whitley county who I didn't recognize, and Ken Sagan from Tates Creek High School in Lexington.

A little before the mile mark, I was running right behind Jude when the course went through a little gulley and he tripped and fell. He swore a few choice words, and I knew he would bounce right back up so there wasn't really anything I could do to help him. I stepped around him without losing any momentum and ran a little further before glancing over my shoulder to see where he was and to take a look at who was still with us.

Without even realizing it, and without making a conscious decision about it, I found myself with a ten yard lead just before the halfway point in the Kentucky State Championship. It was as close to an ideal situation for my racing style as I could have asked for in my wildest dreams. In the sport of cross-country, there is no unwritten rule about waiting for a competitor who slips to the ground, or falls behind because he isn't at 100%. The other runners in the pack saw Jude slip, and it seemed like they hesitated in deciding whether to make a surge or just keep hanging on to the place they had in what they knew was going to be a good showing. For whatever reason, they slowed down long enough for me to open a small gap.

I remember thinking "It's now or never" and "Don't do anything stupid" at about the same time. I put in one small surge and opened up another 10 yards to put me 20 yards ahead of the closest follower. The course made another sharp right-hand turn, so I glanced out of my peripheral vision to see the next five or six runners starting to spread out into a single file behind me. This is usually a sign runners are hurting to a point where their willingness to push ahead is starting to evaporate. Billy Moorman was immediately behind me and three or four places behind him was Jude, who seemed to be still running strong. The real race was on.

Throughout the next quarter mile I continued to push the pace and continued to spread out the field. The final half mile was one long straightaway and I would not be able to see anyone without turning completely around to look, so I knew if I was going to have a chance of winning I would have to have a thirty or forty yard cushion before we got to the last six hundred yards. I pushed as hard as I possibly could.

Just as I was beginning to feel the pain of my second acceleration in this race, Moorman suddenly came up beside me. I was shocked to first hear him gaining on me and then to look over and actually see him pull up beside me because I was at full throttle and barely thirty seconds before this, I had had a decent lead on him.

I didn't panic, first because I still had something left, and second because I was aware that he must have put a huge amount of effort into catching me. This must have taken something out of him, and my thought was reinforced when he settled into a pace matching mine where he must have slowed down compared to the speed he was running to catch me. The back of my head was starting to get numb, and my legs were beginning to feel heavy. There were still three quarters of a mile left. My breathing was starting to get out of rhythm, but I felt like I still had another gear left for the last quarter mile. We ran side by side for only about 100 yards before we made the last turn where we could see all the way to the finish. It would only be another minute or so before we entered the long gauntlet of spectators

270

JUGGERNAUTS

stretched out in front of the finish chute.

The volume of the cheering crowd was amazingly loud, though I could not make out the words or tell who was being cheered for. For no other reason I can think of than that I had completely spent myself from the beginning of the race and the several accelerations I had made to put myself in this position, with about 500 yards to go to the finish, my body pretty much locked up. Almost like a bad dream, Moorman was at first a stride ahead of me, and then with each successive step, he seemed to gain a yard. From my point of view, it was like I was going in reverse while he was speeding away. In reality, it was just him putting on an amazing finishing kick while I staggered and stumbled to the finish line in near complete exhaustion.

My conscious thoughts of the last thirty seconds of the race and the first few minutes afterwards are pretty much lost to the lactic acid dungeons, but people told me later that I did at least put up a fight when he went by me, that we were both flying. It didn't feel like it to me, since all I could think of at the time was that I had lost, but I know I put 100% of what I had on that day into the race. He just flat out beat me and I was quick to acknowledge it to him even though both of us were wobbly and near passing out when we shook hands at the end of the finish chute.

Billy Moorman ran 10:07 and I had finished in 10:20 on a muddy, slippery course, narrowly escaping the pack of runners who were gaining on me every step of the last 100 yards.

Two seconds behind me came the third place runner, Dennis Creekmore from Whitley County, and then within the next thirteen seconds the next seven runners came along with only the 8th and 10th place finishers being from the same school – Apollo High from Owensboro. Jude had truly performed miraculously well to finish 13th in 10:38, considering how he felt and suffering not just one, but two falls on the course.

As I regained my breath and could focus my attention to something besides standing upright, I tried to do the simple math of figuring out whether our team had won or not. Owensboro had placed several runners in the top twenty and only Jude and I had made that cut from our team. When there are no obviously dominant teams, anything can happen when you start adding up the scores. Our third senior, Denny Heidrich, had the race of his life to finish 22nd in 10:49, with Gerry Baynum 26th in 10:51, and John 29th in 10:53.

As each of them finished and carried their finish card to Coach, I added the numbers in my head: 2, 13, 22, 26, 29 – a total of 92 points. My first thought was that there was no way a score that high would win the State Meet, since off the top of my head, I remember seeing several tightly bunched runners from other schools coming through the finish.

What I did not take into account in my rough version of the scoring was that the final results take out the individual entrants in the race who are not part of a full team. Since these runners are obviously some of the top individuals, there can be large reductions in the team scores after all of this is sorted out.

Coach Daley had several assistants attempting to tally the final score, but we were not able to make any early determination of our team's placing since we did not have the exact placing of any of our competitor's runners.

Normally in cross-country, the coaches are able to perform a calculation that arrives at the winner well before the final tally is made by the meet officials. In this race, the team placings were so close and the individuals affecting the scoring were such a big part of the equation that not one of the coaches knew ahead of time what the final outcome would be.

When the final runner came in several minutes later, the meet officials took their results papers into the tent set up behind the finish area and made their final calculations. This took an inordinate amount of time and maybe they wanted to add some drama to the day's festivities – because they certainly took their time about tallying the final results. By the time they were finished calculating the team scores, they were ready to begin handing out the awards for the individuals and decided to withhold the team scores until they handed out the trophies.

In the agonizing half hour before they began announcing the winners, I had recovered enough to put on my sweats, go around and congratulate my teammates and competitors on their efforts, find my girlfriend and parents and accept their hugs and congratulations on my race, and do a easy loop of the course as a warmdown.

I had an uneasy feeling that we had not performed well enough to win and I had made up my mind to be a gracious looser if that was the way it turned out. After receiving my individual award for second place, and standing on the podium while the State Champion Billy Moorman accepted his gold medal, I rejoined my teammates while we all awaited the team champion announcement.

Jude was still pretty sick. After wobbling around for some time after the finish, he had recovered enough to be nervous with the rest of us. Rumors had spread that we had finished second. Other rumors spread that we had won. Coach said, just wait until they announce it because nobody knew anything and besides everybody was going to find out soon.

After stepping to the podium with his paper and seemingly ready to begin announcing the final results, the meet

273

STEVE ADKISSON

official walked back to the scorer's table and had several people there lean over his shoulder and look at the paper. Apparently satisfied with the answers he was given, he returned to the microphone and began his announcement.

"In third place, with a total of 109 points Paducah Tilman High School."

A loud applause came up from an area off to our right and the seven runners came forward to accept their trophy and stood while a few pictures were taken. They started to walk away.

My heart skipped a few beats. I licked my lips.

"Stay up here a minute gentlemen. We want to get everyone's picture before you leave." The Paducah team reassembled to the side of the podium.

"In second place, with a total team score of 78 points . .

I had the number "92" locked in my mind and the instant I heard "78" I became totally deflated as I knew that beat our score. My mind raced through several quick scenarios and before I could come to a conclusion, the meet official answered mine and everyone else's question.

"Owensboro High School."

This time there were two separate groups who erupted in applause and whoops and jumping up and down. John grabbed me in a great bear hug and jumped up with me in his arms. Jude, Gerry, Denny, J.C., and Jeff were each high fiving and laughing and we were each smiling a smile that seldom happens on this earth – the smile of satisfied joy. Coach Daley acted like he didn't know whether to laugh or cry and I think for a minute he might have been doing both at the same time. He shook hands all around, and was just beaming when the meet official finally got around to announcing the final results.

"And our 1975 Kentucky State Class AA Champions,

274

with a score of 70 points, a repeat winner from last year, the Lloyd Memorial High School Juggernauts."

This time, there was not only the applause from the many fans from Erlanger who had come to watch the meet, but from the entire crowd of cross-country fans, our competitors, and the coaches. I caught the eye of Billy Moorman as our team walked up to accept our trophy, and he smiled a great big smile at me while he clapped his hands and nodded his head up and down. It was just this kind of sportsmanship and respect which had drawn me four years ago to this sport and I smiled back and nodded and pointed a reciprocal finger back at him.

We accepted the trophy and happily stood for some pictures and shook hands all around again with the other runners.

Coach Daley carried the trophy back out to where there was a big gathering of our families and friends and passed it all around while hugs from parents, and kisses from girlfriends, and handshakes from friends were passed around. If there was anything different from the feeling of winning last year, it was quite simply a deeper sense of accomplishment than anything I could have imagined. The pain and fatigue of the race had vanished and had been replaced with a feeling of elation that was shared among this large community of supporters.

Winning is not everything, but it is right up there. We had earned this victory and all of the good feelings which go along with it. It had cost us a lot but in the hours and days afterwards, the price seemed a bargain. We were honored in so many ways, it got to be almost embarrassing for me. We were recognized in a special pep rally at school. We were taken to a banquet for "State Champions." We were guests on an A.M. sport's radio show again, interviewed by newspaper reporters, and known throughout the community. I did not really enjoy much of this recognition but tolerated it as part of being on the team, and my teammates for the most part felt the same way. We knew without being told that winning was just the natural conclusion to living a life fully dedicated to the simple principle of doing everything you know to do to be the best you can be. Some things go without saying.

Team Photo 1975.

Just about the time things were settling down to normal and we had started back to daily running in preparation for track season, we were confronted with one of the biggest surprises of any we could have imagined. Without giving much thought to it, a few weeks had gone by without Coach Daley being at practice. We chalked this up to him needing some time off after the four hard months of the season and the weeklong celebration following the State Meet. We had grown up enough to be able to organize ourselves to meet after school to run when we were 'out-of-season'. It was something that had become second nature for those of us who were serious about running. So when Coach came into the locker room on the Monday after

Thanksgiving, it took us by surprise.

He looked around the locker room taking inventory of who was there. He said he'd like to see all of the seniors in his office in such a serious tone that we all looked at each other wondering which of the many things we might have done had finally caught up to us.

We followed him into his little office at the back of the locker room.

He said "Wait here a minute," and went back out.

He came back in leading John, Gerry, Jeff, & J.C. - the varsity members of the team who were not seniors.

There were only three chairs in the room so all of us had our backs up against the walls, standing with our arms crossed and heads bowed in preparation for the anticipated tongue lashing we were about to get.

"Fellas, I have something I want to tell you," he began.

I had known Coach Daley for four years and had almost daily contact with him through some of the best and worst times of my life. He had never felt obliged to preface anything he was going to say with a redundant phrase like this.

"I have been offered and I have accepted a college coaching job at Northern Kentucky State College, which will become Northern Kentucky University next year. I will start there the first of the year so I will be leaving Lloyd at the end of December. I want you to know this has nothing to do with how I feel about any of you. We have had some of the best times of my life here together. It is because of our success here that I was offered this position.

"This is an opportunity for me and my family I felt like I could not pass up. I know it is sudden and I have been working with the school administration here to arrange that Mr. Hinsdale will continue to coach you through the track season and he has committed to coach cross-country next year. He will do a great job for you and I know you will

277

have a great track season with or without me because you are in remarkable shape already.

"Because I am going to be NCAA coach, I can't really say anything today, but I would hope some of you who are seniors will want to come to Northern next year. You would all be welcome and I hope to know more about the scholarship situation there. We can talk about it later.

"I will of course always be available to you. You know where I live, you have my telephone number. My door is always open. If there is anything at all I can do for any of you, just let me know."

He had spilled this all out and I don't think even one of us was prepared for this of the infinite possible reasons he had asked us into his office. We all stood silently absorbing this and when Coach paused for the obvious offering of a time to ask questions, we were all too stunned to speak.

"Does anybody have any questions?" he asked.

No one did.

"Well, don't let me hold you up," he said, and he said it in way indicating a little bit of disappointment and a little bit of sadness which made me feel bad that I didn't take the opportunity to express how I really felt about it. Each of us had our own internal conversations going on, yet no one could muscle up more than a "Thanks Coach" as we filed out the door into the cold rain for a six mile run.

JUGGERNAUTS

Cincinnati Enquirer 12/12/1975
Kentucky Sports – Herb Whitney
"Give Credit To The Kids, Coach Daley Says"

Mike Daley, the coach, graciously credits his athletes for his success.

"I was fortunate to have quite a few dedicated Kids," said Daley. "They deserve the credit."

Steve Adkisson, the runner, begs to disagree with his former taskmaster.

"That isn't true at all," Adkisson said. "We might've been able to win the state this year without him. Probably not, though.

Daley coached cross-country at Erlanger Lloyd for four seasons. His runners, including Adkisson, brought home the last two state Class AA championships.

Daley has decided to change jobs, however, and early next month he will become the cross-country coach and trainer at Northern Kentucky State College.

Will Lloyd miss Daley?

"We sure will," said Adkisson, who like many of his cross-country teammates will compete in track this spring without Daley as their coach. "It'll be hard for the runners who are coming back next fall."

Daley delayed any formal announcement of his new job until he had met with his runners and explained his reasons for going.

"I owed them that much," Daley said. "It wasn't something they should pick up from the local newspaper. I was concerned they'd think I abandoned them for a college job. So I was honest with them the way I've always been."

Daley stressed one thing while telling his runners of the move.

STEVE ADKISSON

"I didn't want them thinking that from now on our relationship was through," he said. "I told them I'm still available anytime they want to call me or drop by the house."

. . .

How does Daley sum up his accomplishments at Lloyd, a school that was mediocre in cross-country before his arrival in 1972?

"I always saw my position there as the chance to give kids some pride through a sport, and pride in a sport," Daley said. "No one at Lloyd considered cross-country a sport when I arrived there. It was just a conditioner for basketball.

"My biggest accomplishment, I guess, was helping runners realize that cross-country is an important sport in its own right. We succeeded. Pretty soon almost every kid we had just ran cross-country and track. It was no longer a conditioner.

"I hate to leave Lloyd. Everyone there has been good to me. Especially the runners. They deserve all the credit."

JUGGERNAUTS

"Though the many beings are numberless
I vow to save them
Though greed, hatred, and ignorance rise endlessly
I vow to end them
Though the path is vast and fathomless
I vow to understand it
Though enlightenment is beyond attainment
I vow to embody it fully"

-Bodhisattva Vow

The possum rolled over and pretended to be asleep. Actually it seemed more like pretending to not want to bite you but just waiting for the right opportunity. Denny exceeded his previously measured vertical leaping ability by about two feet and I set a P.R. for side jumping while thinking which of a dozen curse words best fit the situation. As an aspiring poet, I'd begun developing the habit of not giving in to the first word that popped into my head, so as I began my descent above the possum, I searched the vast resources at my disposal and came up with the word "aaaaiiiisshheeeitfire." It was the best I could do under the circumstances.

What had begun as a grinding miserable run in the dark winter night had suddenly become something altogether different. When our fear subsided and we stood looking at the curled up possum, we were both giddy with the adrenaline that running quietly through the night on a dark street and suddenly encountering the hiss and instant sleep of the lone surviving marsupial in Kentucky can inspire.

We stood looking alternately at each other and the possum, each other and the scruffy fur, each other and the teeth, each other and the. . .

Neither of us had to say it. You don't know somebody since second grade, run thousands of miles beside them, spend hundreds of nights hanging out, and have to say out loud what absolutely anybody in our particular situation would just about have to do with this possum.

This winter run was one of our first since the Christmas break and it had all the conditions that explain why most normal people don't run outside much between Halloween and Easter. A brisk wind was coming out of the north. It was about twenty degrees. I'm sure there was some basketball game on the TV. We had homework to do. We had girls to call on the phone, laundry waiting to be washed, rooms to clean, cars to repair. If you've been seventeen, you know all the options.

All I know is when Denny called me and said "Hadley, we're going for a run," I was dressed and out the door in three minutes and met him at the same corner we always met when he called.

The standard course from the corner headed a mile up the two lane road toward Dixie Highway. From there we had the choice of crossing the highway over the railroad trestle, turning left at the highway and heading up toward the high school, or turning right and down the highway towards Chinatown and the Food Mart.

It just so happened that on this particular evening, our accumulated Karma (this fact I haven't learned until much later in life, though I did have the inner understanding at a young age) had brought us toe to nose with the marsupial. This cosmic occurrence happened within sight of the train trestle where a route decision would have to be made. Out and back courses went against any running etiquette yet invented and as we stood there, our path was determined for us.

"Jude working tonight?" Denny asked me.

"Six to ten," I said.

"What time is it?"

"It was nine thirty when I left my house."

Jude was the best runner on our team for the entire season. He was our best friend. He had a blue 69 Camaro, three-speed on the column, with at this moment no functioning battery. Which meant he had to park it facing downhill and kick start it every time he needed it to run. He worked at the Food Mart, the town's largest grocery store. The Camaro didn't have working door locks and seemed a very likely place to deposit the possum. If we could get it there.

Being absolutely a cold natured, minimum body fat endurance athlete, I had on as many layers of sweat clothes, socks, and gloves as I could run with. In the days before Gore-tex and polypropylene, this was a considerable number of layers. Enough so that I wasn't afraid of getting bit through them. I pulled my outer gloves, which were really nothing but my older brother's leather work gloves anyway, on tighter and bent over the possum. When I put my hand out to see what would happen, it hissed and showed its interlocking row of puncturing fangs. I slid one gloved hand behind its head and the other under his rear-end. I picked him up and was surprised both at how much it weighed and how docile it seemed.

I know cross training has come a long way since 1975, but there's something uniquely challenging in carrying a twelve-pound possum at 5:40 mile pace down a dark city street. Food Mart is only about a half mile down the highway from the trestle and I still hold the record for this distance in the marsupial baton division.

Denny opened the passenger side door and I slid the critter on to the floor. It was hard to contain our enthusiasm, but a moment like this is the perfect time to work on your poker face so we thought we'd go in to see Jude. He was back in the baked goods section, stocking Little Debbies, and doing a fabulous job as far as we could tell. We strode casually down the aisle and said "Hello".

He said "Hey! What the . . ? You guys out running?"

Denny said we were grocery shopping and pretended to be looking for something on a shelf.

"Hey, get this," Denny said. "We just saw these two guys from Boone County running down the highway."

"What, them pansies out in this weather?" Jude said.

"I reckon so."

He was a little better at his poker face than I was, but I just stood there with that silly grin that doesn't really mean much to somebody until sometime later. I said we just stopped by to let him know we were getting in our "secret miles," something each of us accused the other of in situations when one of us had to work, had a date, or their old man was making them mow the lawn while the rest of us were out running.

Jude said he would have liked to be out with us, but he wouldn't be off for another fifteen minutes. Denny said we needed to get going before we started sweating. We didn't want to get chilled halfway into our run.

Neither of us said much on the run home. Sometimes there are just too many possibilities to comprehend and the fate of the possum and its soon to be manifested relationship with Jude was one of those mysteries that had too many possibilities to attempt putting into words.

"Check you at school tomorrow," Denny said when we got to his house.

"Catch you later," I said, never breaking stride and ran the rest of the way home in that smiling, elevated state of consciousness many a monk has meditated a lifetime to find.

EPILOGUE

Steve Adkisson accepted a track scholarship to Morehead State University. Following a sophomore year full of overuse injuries, he transferred to Murray State University where he received an academic scholarship. He trained with the Murray State Cross Country and Track Teams while he competed for the Mason Dixon Athletic Club. He continues to run and compete in cross-country, track, duathlon, triathlon, road and ultra marathon trail races.

Mike Daley coached several years at Northern Kentucky University, and developed the first NCAA All American from the university in distance runner John Lott. After several years at NKU, he left coaching and worked in the pharmaceutical industry. He died a tragic early death and is survived by his wife Becky and son John.

AFTERWORD

This is a fairly accurate chronicling of events involving the Lloyd Memorial High School Juggernaut cross country teams during the years 1972-1975. It is rendered through mostly rose colored rear view lenses, so those of you who are featured here may dispute certain factual aspects of this work. Blatant embellishments and gross understatements of events loosely based on the life of the author occur throughout but most outright lies have been removed through several revisions. You be the judge. It is dedicated mostly to Mike Daley, but could not have been possible without the existence of John Adkisson, Jude Baynum, Gerry Baynum, Matt Huff, Steve Nienaber, Mark Rhodes, Gary Graves, J. C. Clayton, Doug Vagedes, Terry Brake, Jeff Ogden, Mark Seyer, Kevin Burlew, Roger Black, Herald Hensley, Dave Crump, and a host of other teammates whose omission here is no indication of my level of appreciation and respect for the goodness your existence added to my life. Thank you all.

Where the *Kentucky Enquirer, Kentucky Post,* or *Louisville Courier-Journal* are quoted, these are exact texts from the papers noted with only minor deletions for brevity's sake.

Some of the other stuff I just made up.

287

All photographs credited with "Spectator Yearbook. Photographer Unknown" are used with the permission of the Erlanger-Elsmere Board of Education. Special thanks to Superintendent Michael Sander and Board attorney Lawson Walker for their generosity in granting this permission. Readers who may know the photographers responsible for these truly remarkable photos are asked to contact the author for noting deserved credit in possible future printings of this book.

Thanks also to Katie Eades, whose superb editing created a much more readable book than the one I asked her to read.

This book is made of words, 100 of which are on the American Heritage Dictionary editors' list of "100 Words Every High School Graduate (And Their Parents) Should Know." For more information on this list, please visit their website.

10 % of all profits from this book will be donated to adult literacy organizations serving the rural south.

To contact author for book signings, speaking engagements, or appearances visit
www.juggernautsthebook.com

Be well. God bless. Run on.

Printed in the United States
131282LV00001B/260/P